SIMON BOND

TEDDY

Methuen

A METHUEN PAPERBACK

First published in Great Britain in 1985
by Methuen London Ltd
11 New Fetter Lane, London EC4P 4EE
Copyright © Polycarp Ltd 1985
Made and printed in Great Britain
by Fletcher & Son Ltd, Norwich

ISBN 0 413 58120 9

With our Great
thanks

Group A3 A101
STIRLING 27/7 | 3/8 1985

[illegible]

Jenny

Jeff [illegible]

Barbara B

Russell.

Rosalie

Pat.

Helen A.

Anne

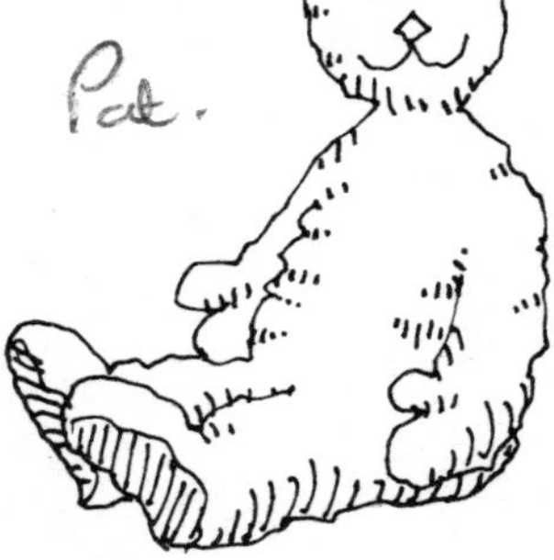

By the same author
A Hundred and One Uses of a Dead Cat
Unspeakable Acts
A Hundred and One More Uses of a Dead Cat
Odd Visions and Bizarre Sights
Success and How To Be One

To Linda

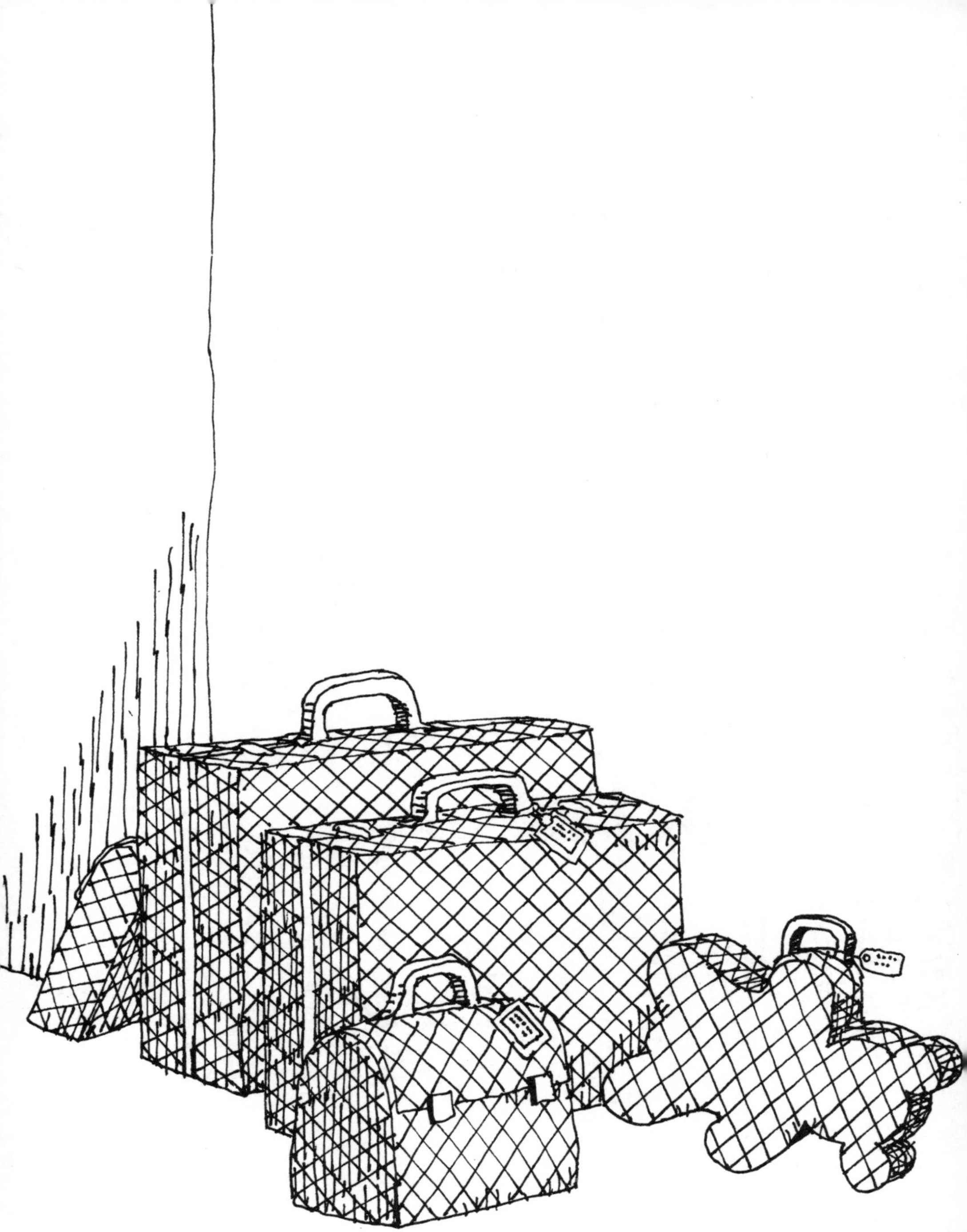

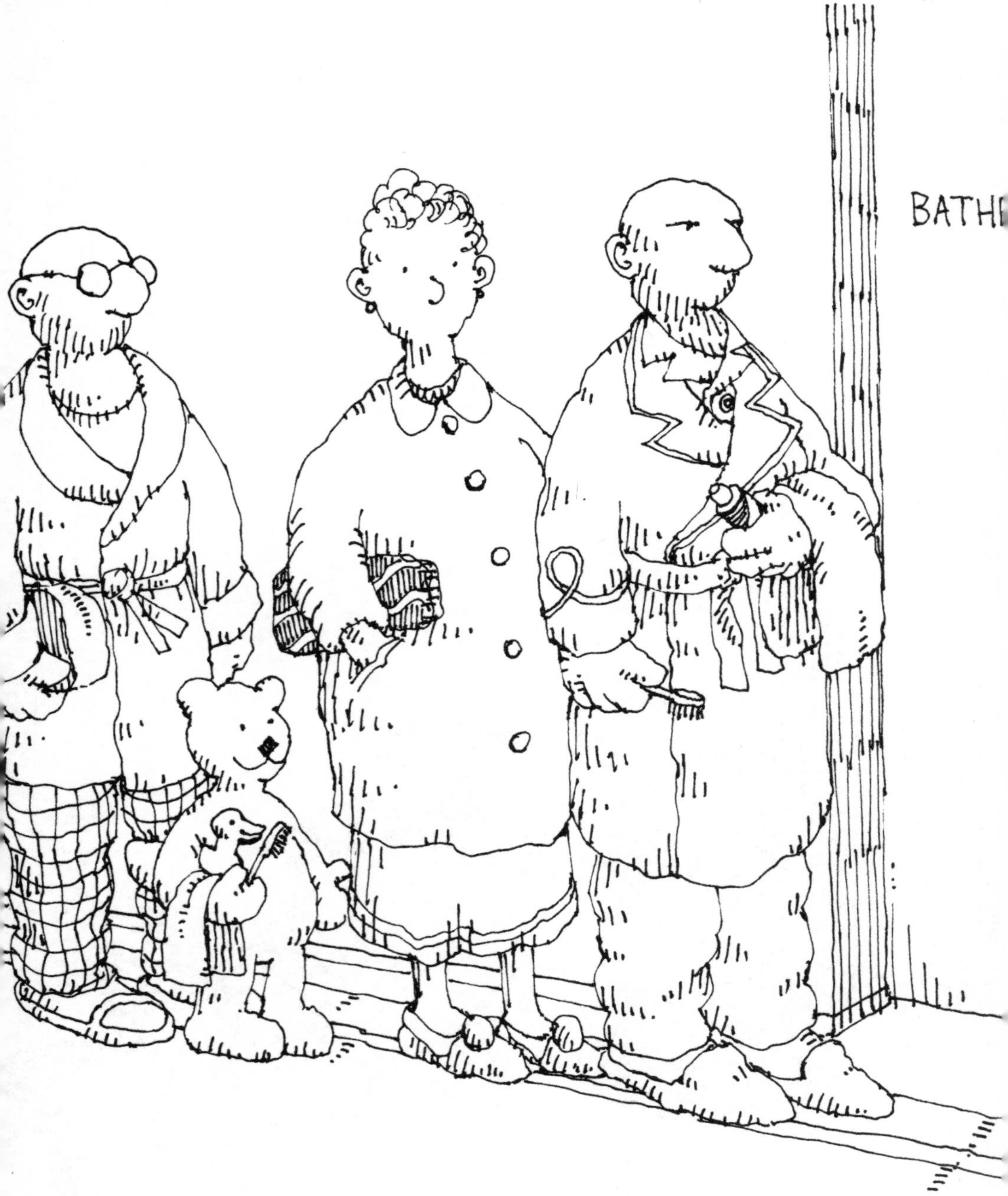
BATH

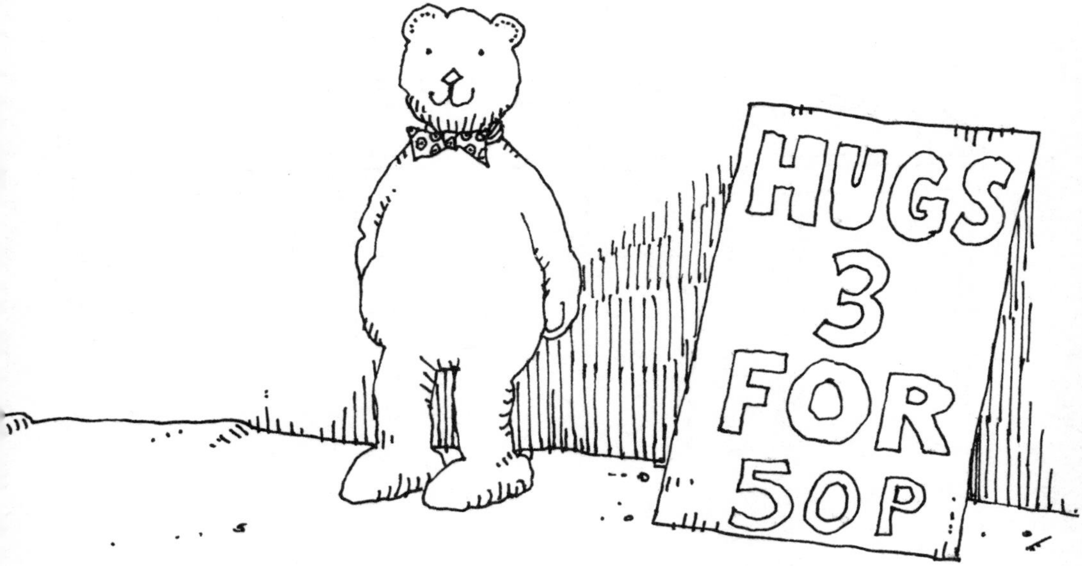
HUGS
3
FOR
50P

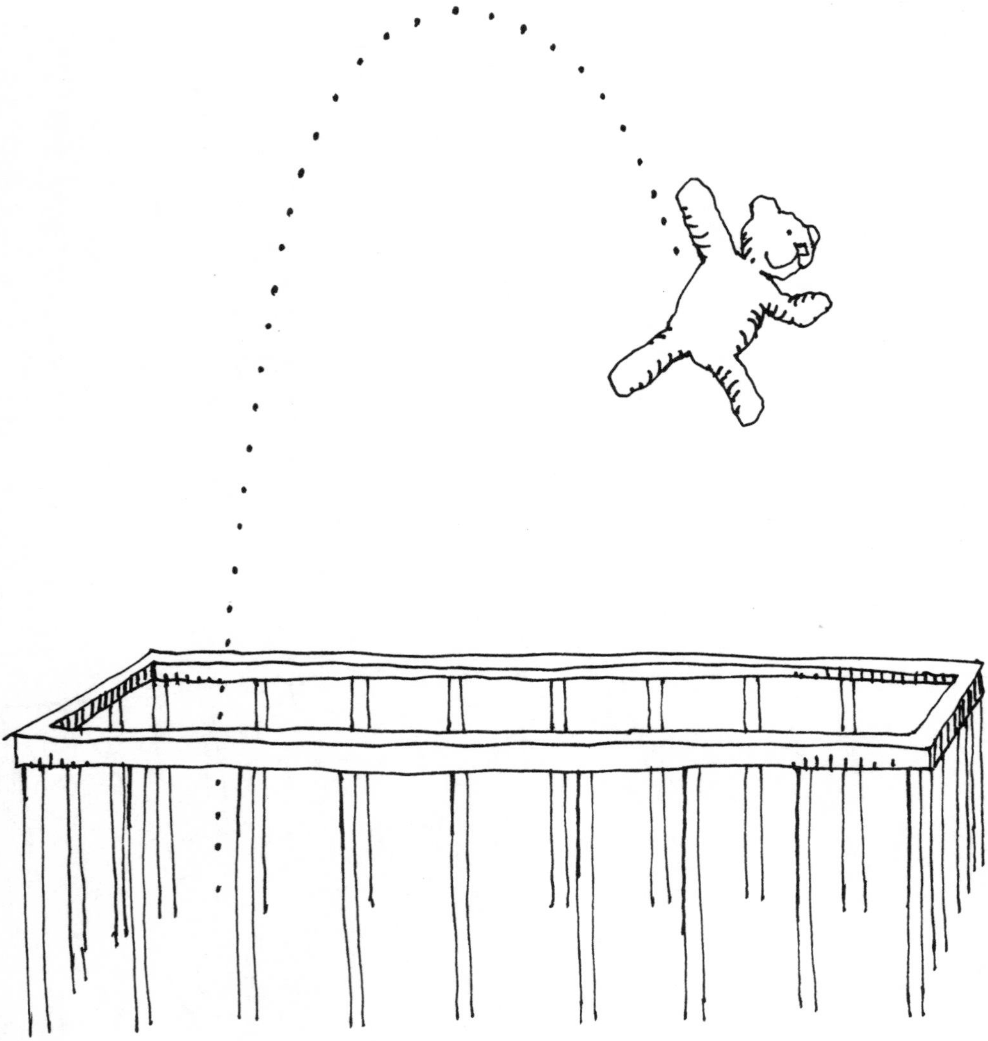

WERNHER VON BRAUN'S
FIRST EXPERIMENT

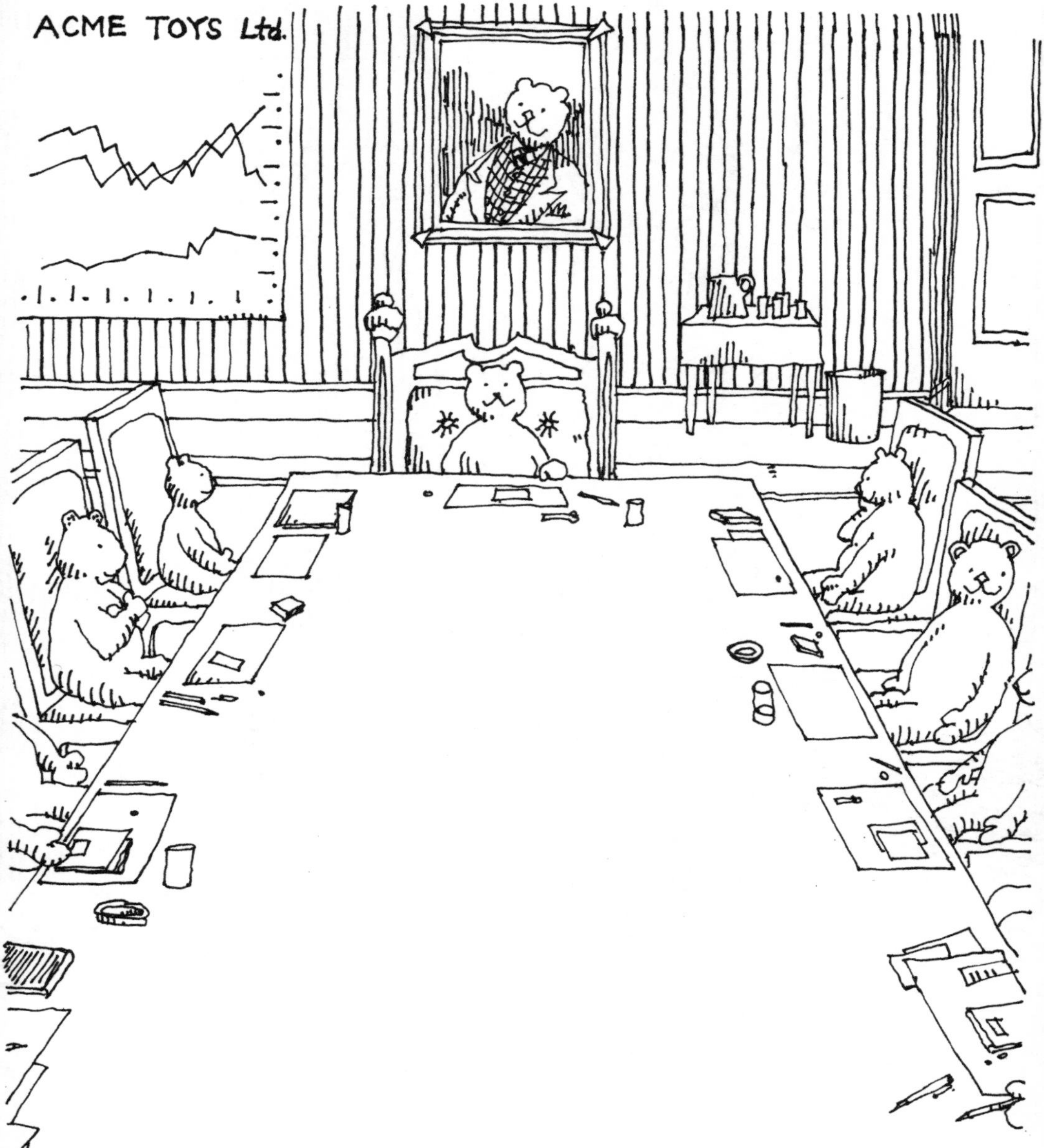
ACME TOYS Ltd.

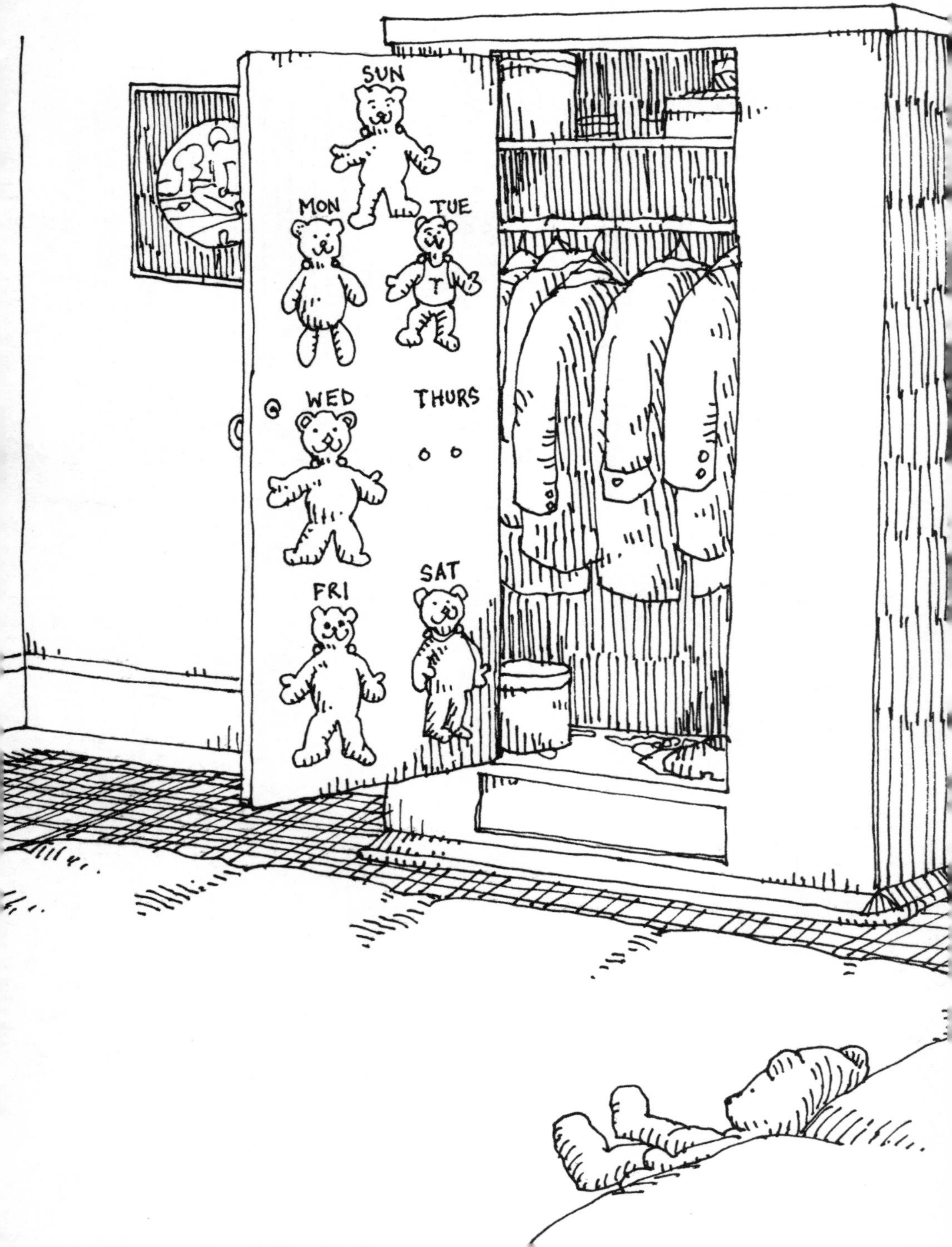
SUN
MON
TUE
WED
THURS
FRI
SAT

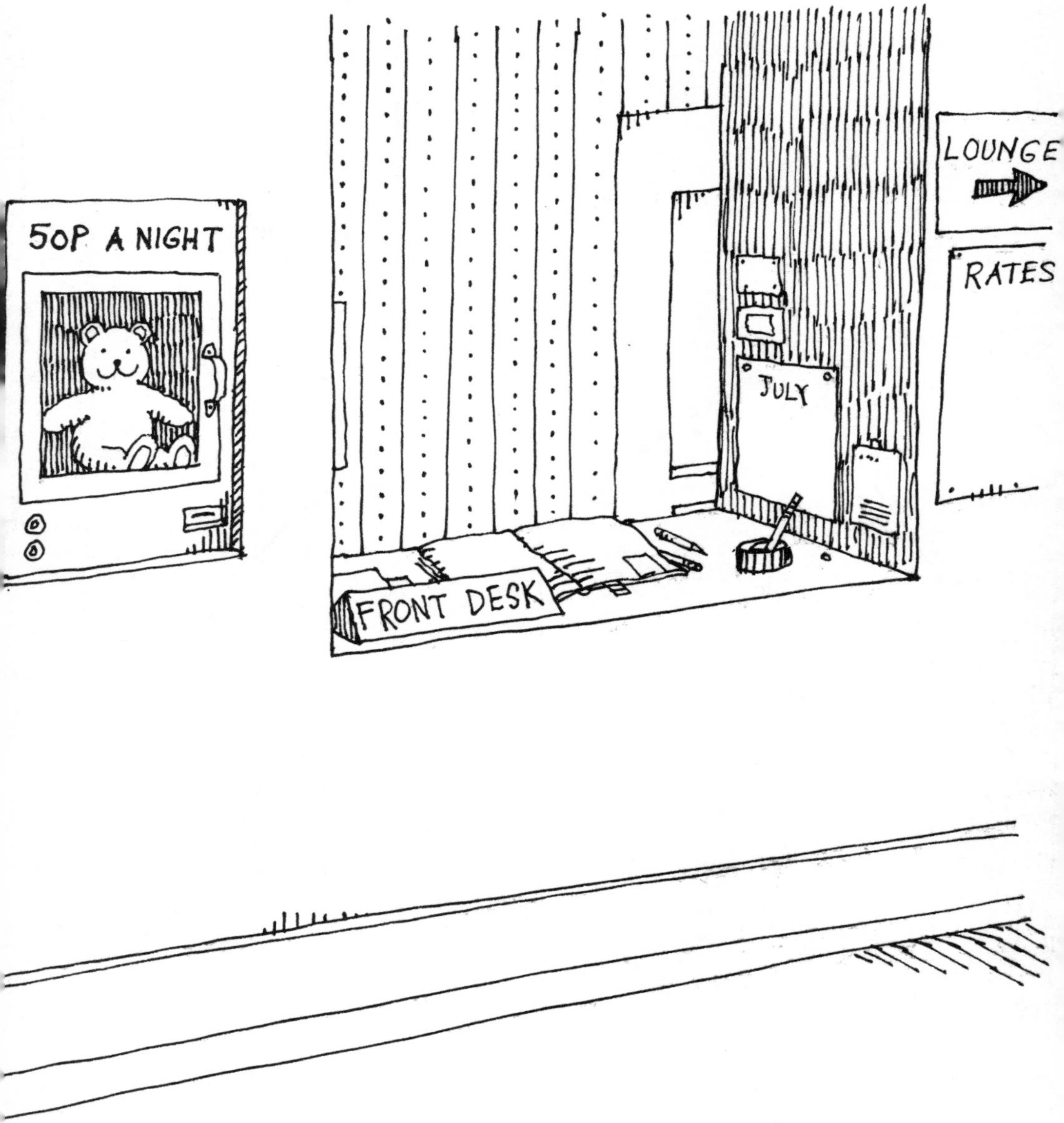

50P A NIGHT
LOUNGE
RATES
JULY
FRONT DESK

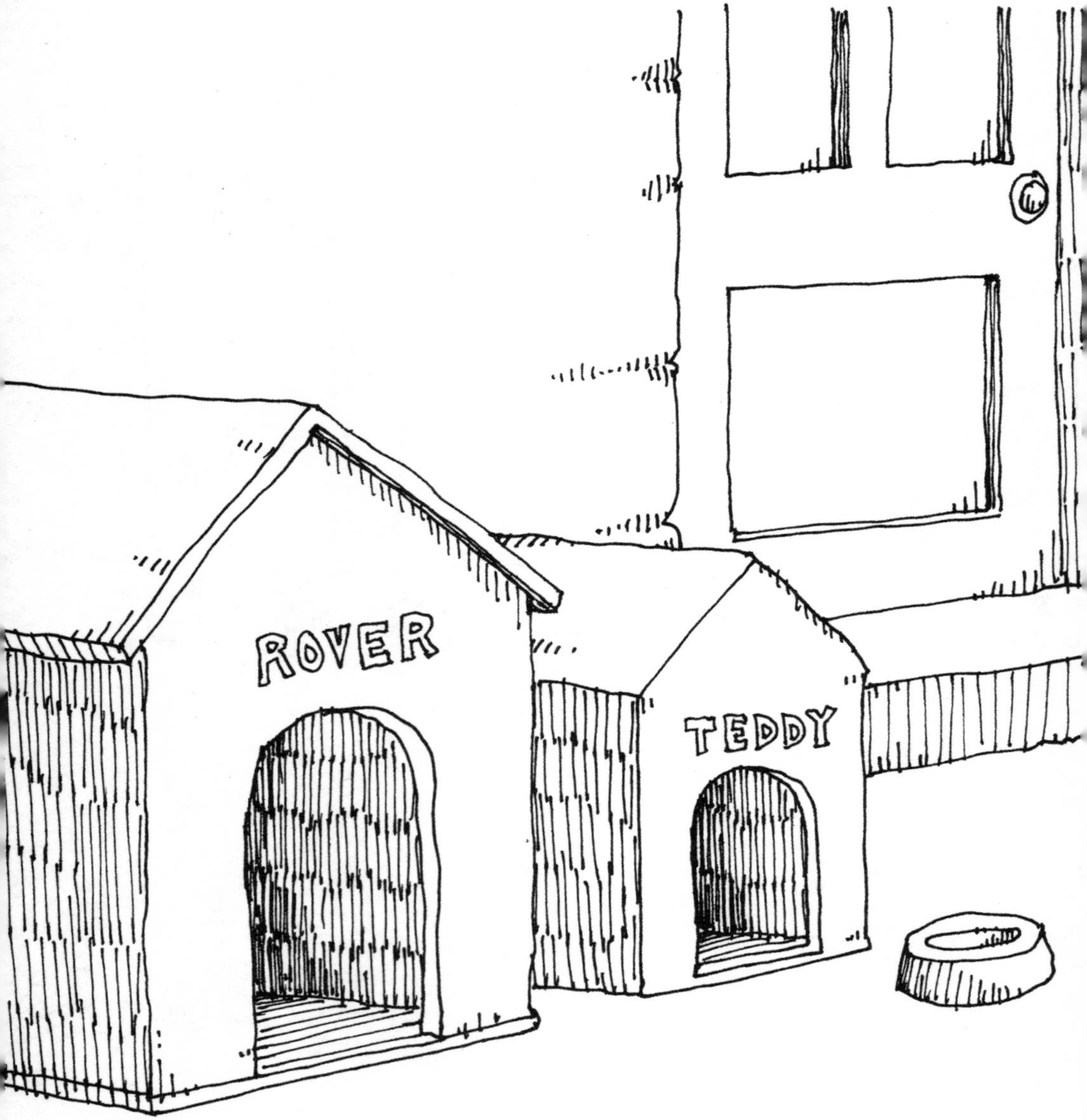
ROVER
TEDDY

TEDDYBEARS IN THE WILD

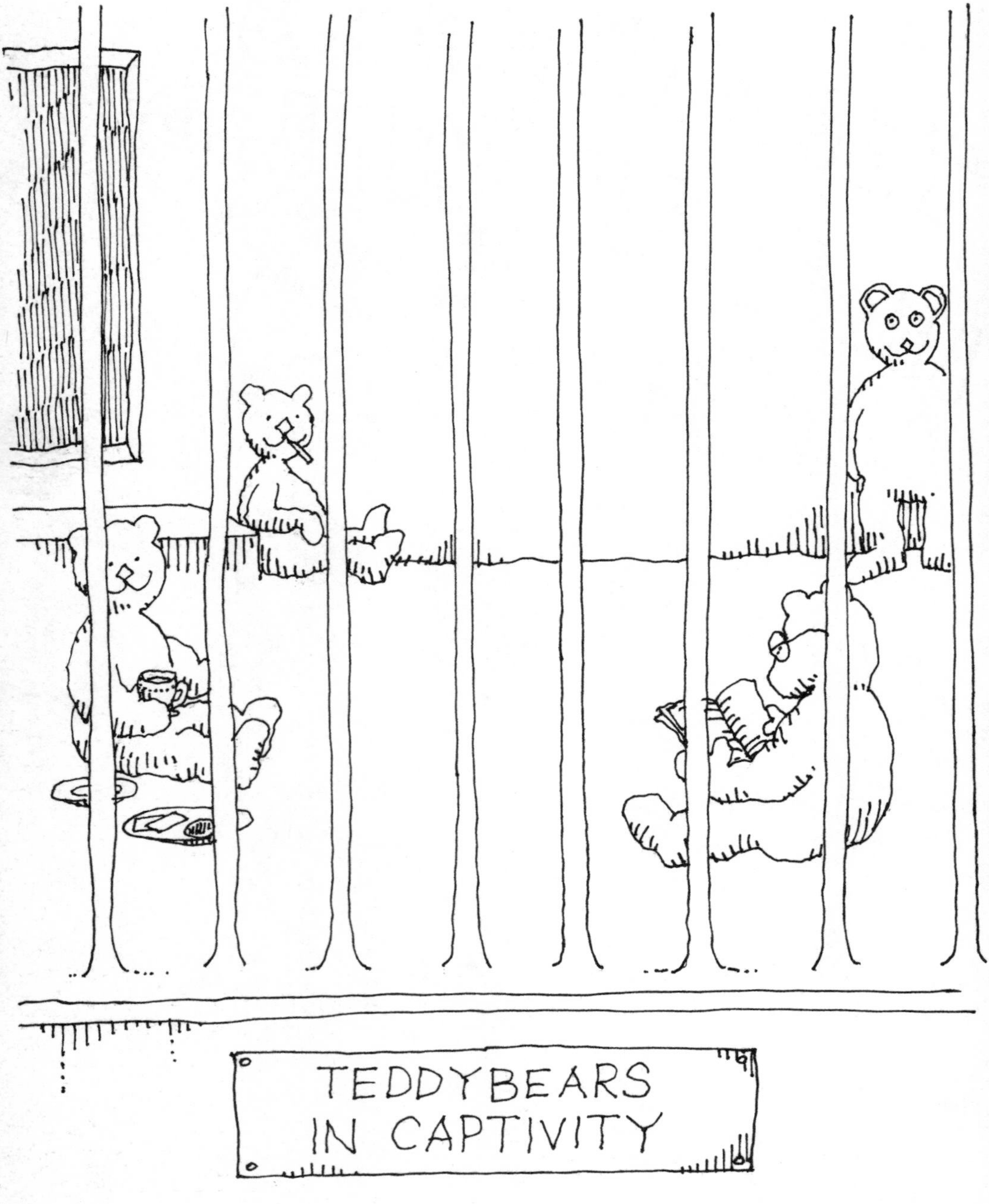
TEDDYBEARS
IN CAPTIVITY

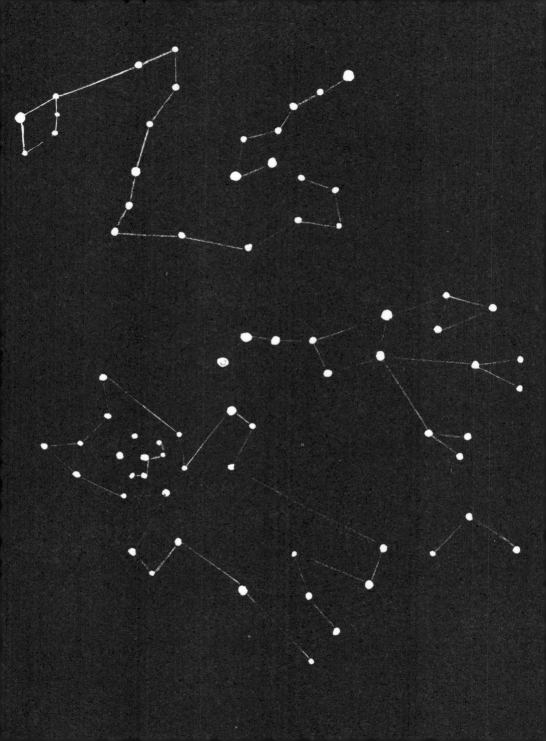

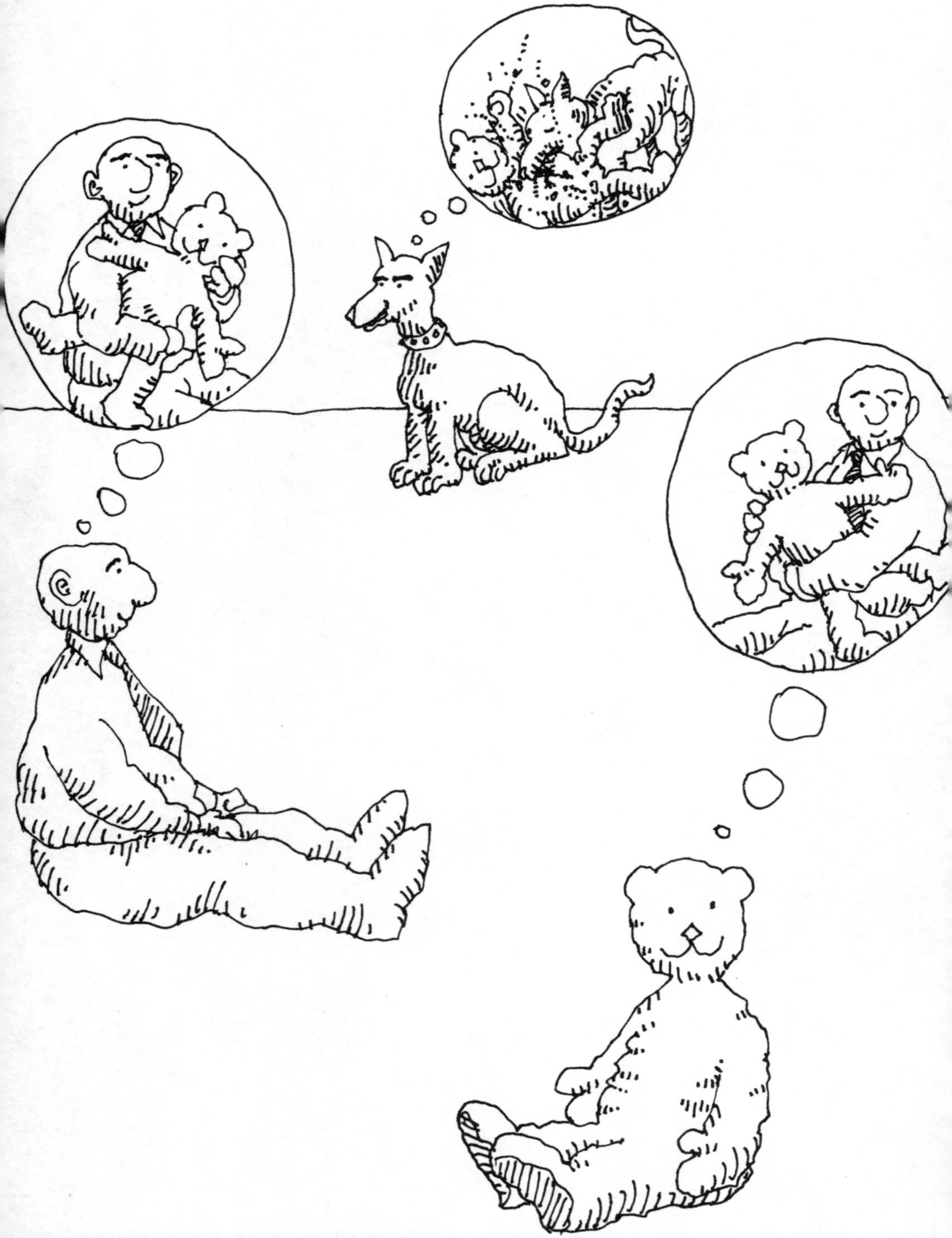

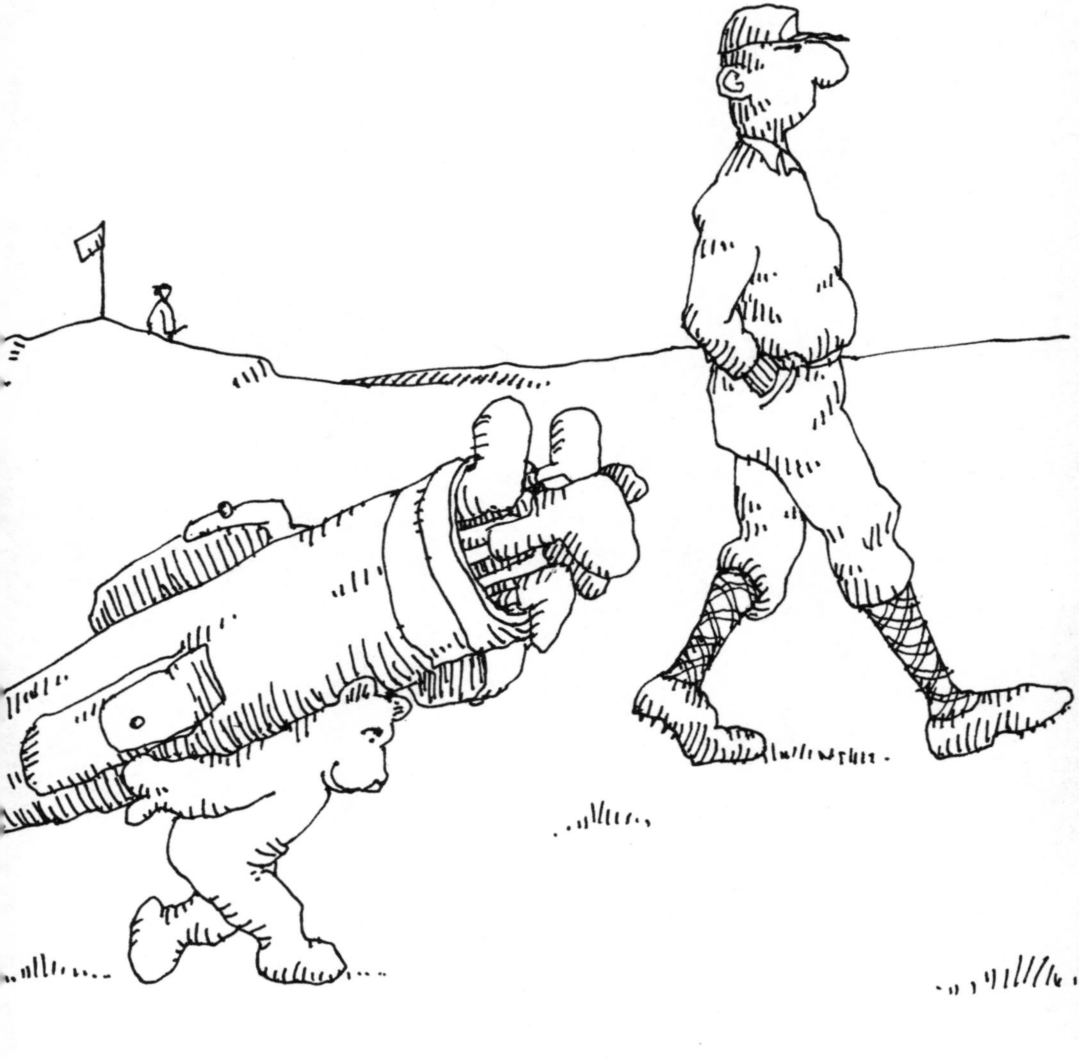

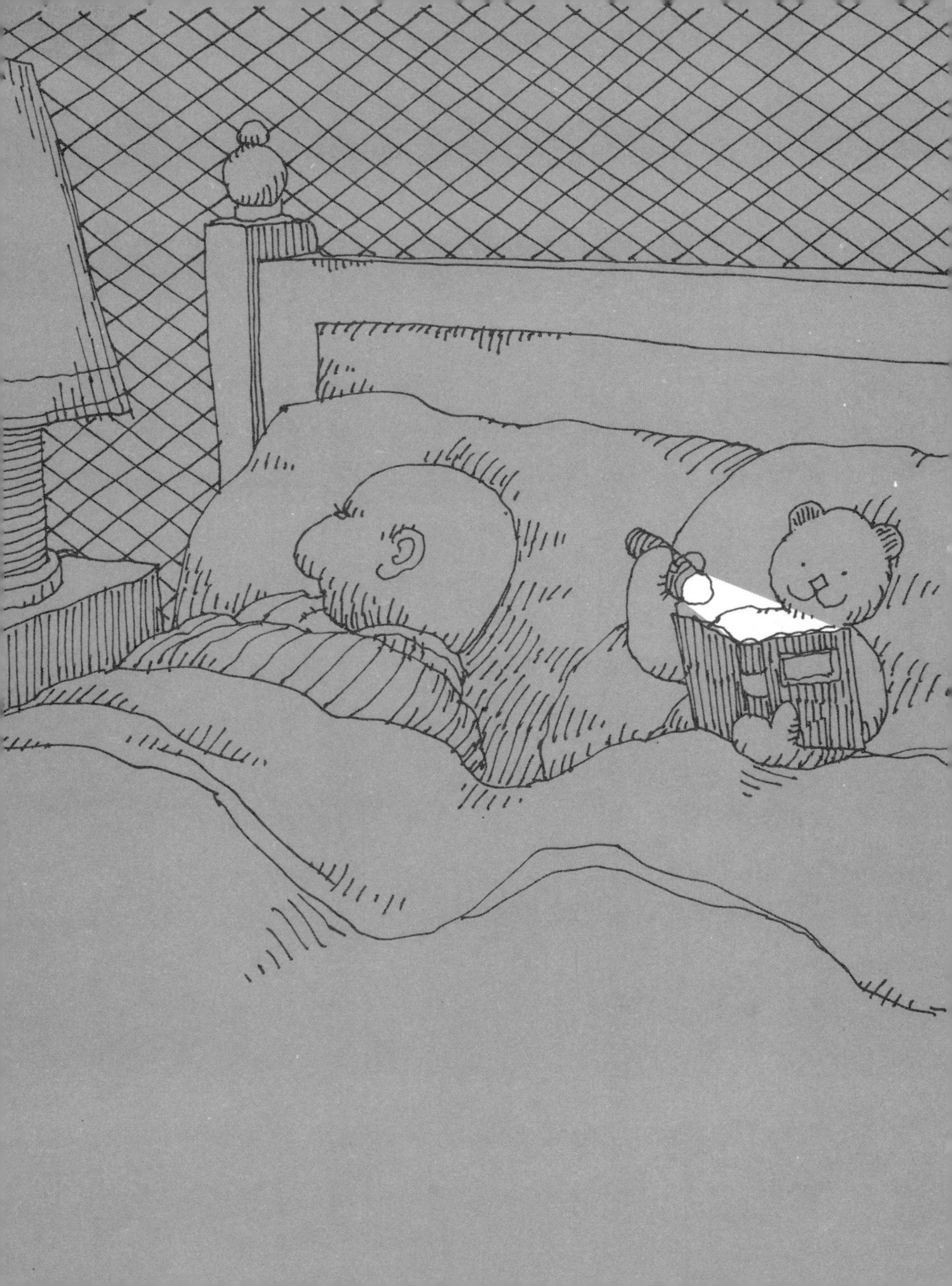

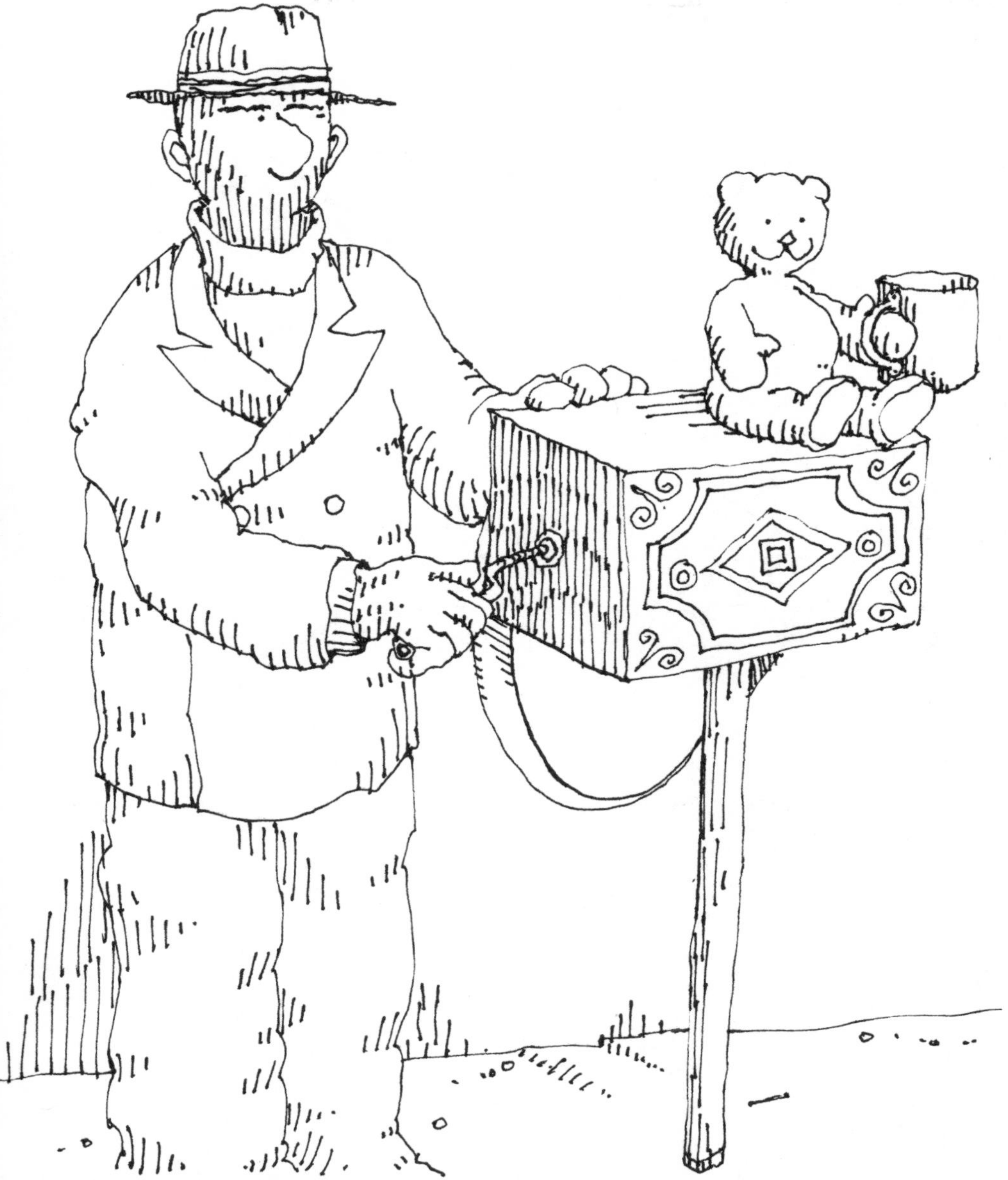

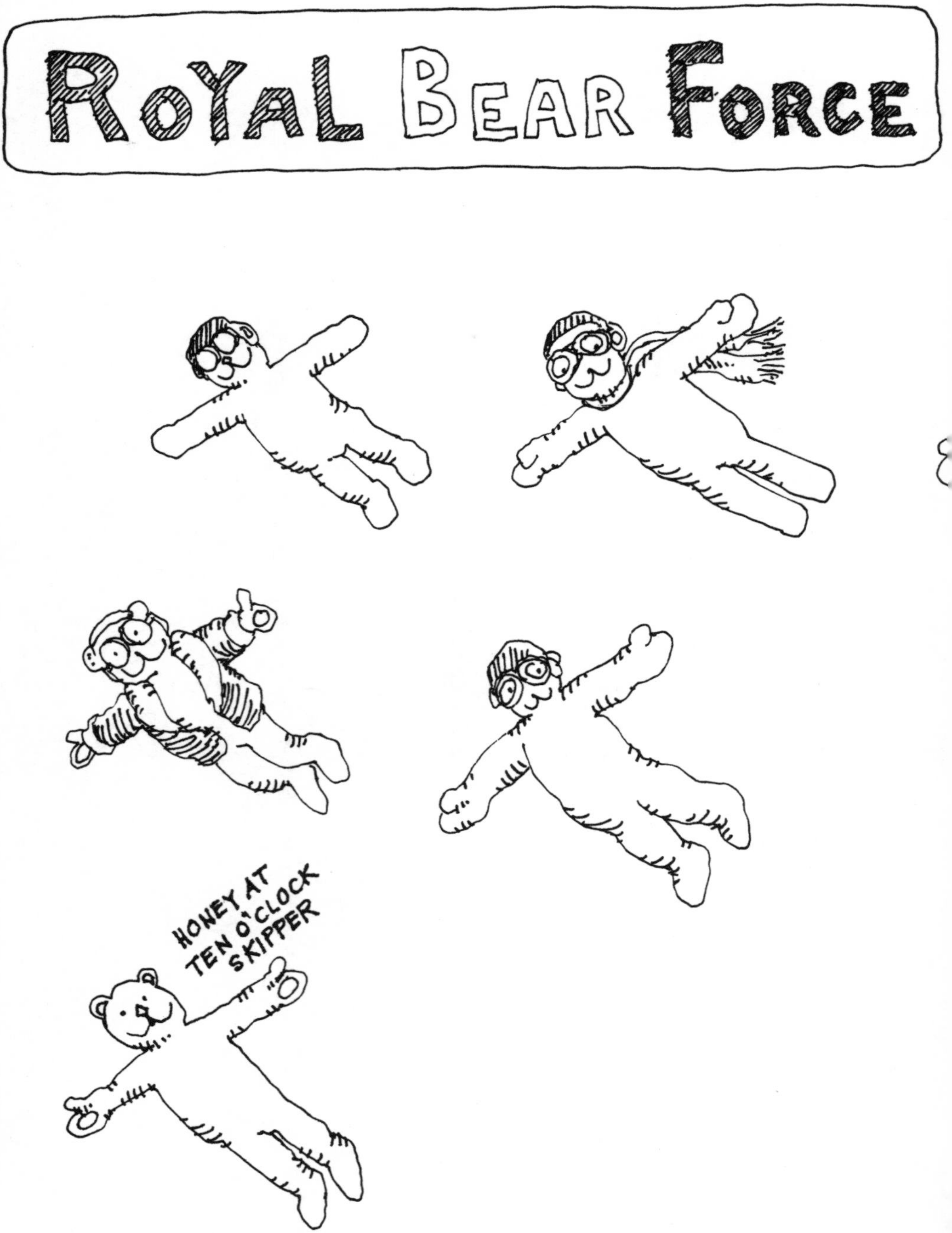
ROYAL BEAR FORCE
HONEY AT TEN O'CLOCK SKIPPER

TEDDYBEARS FOR ALL TRADES

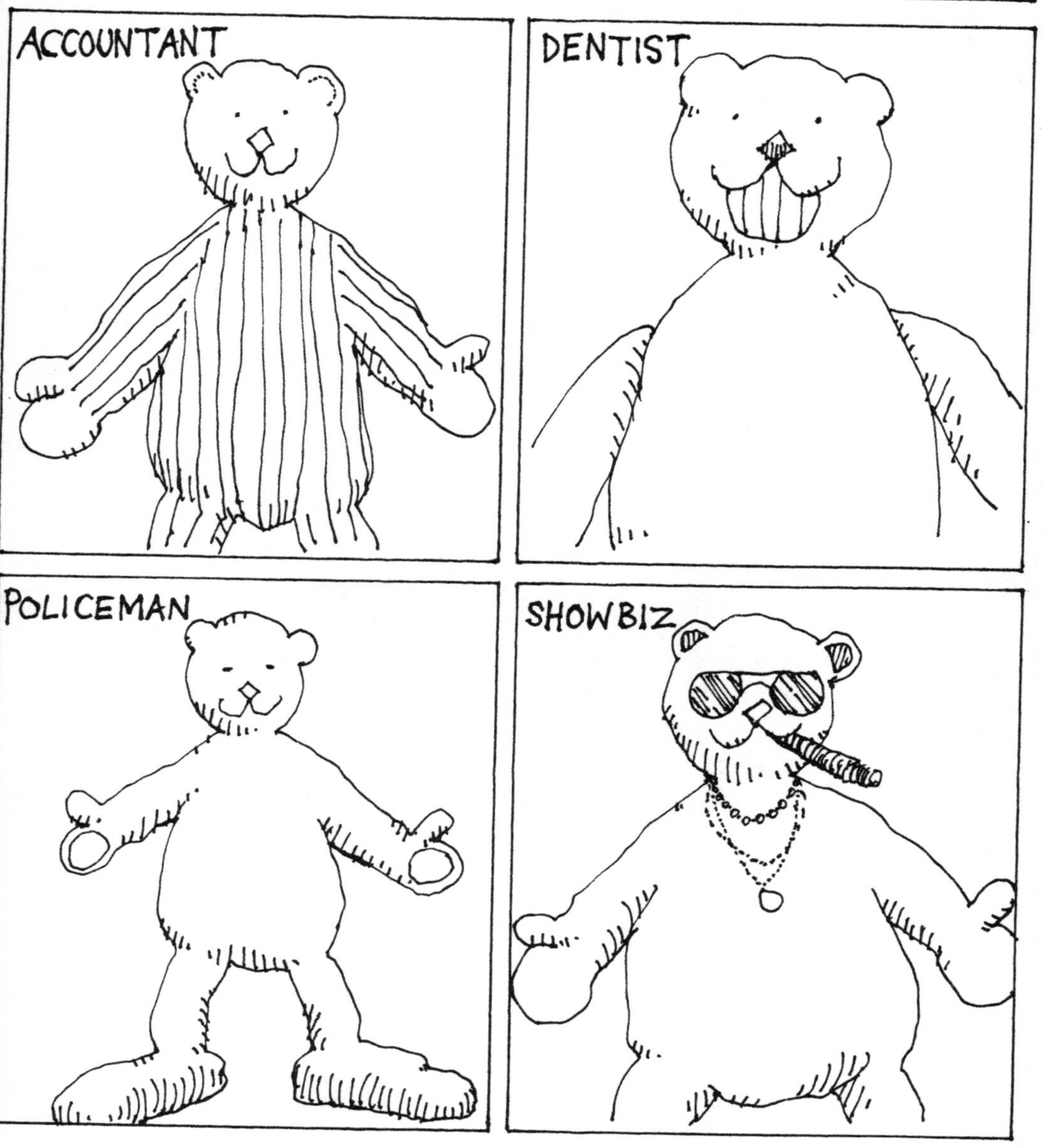

ACCOUNTANT
DENTIST
POLICEMAN
SHOWBIZ

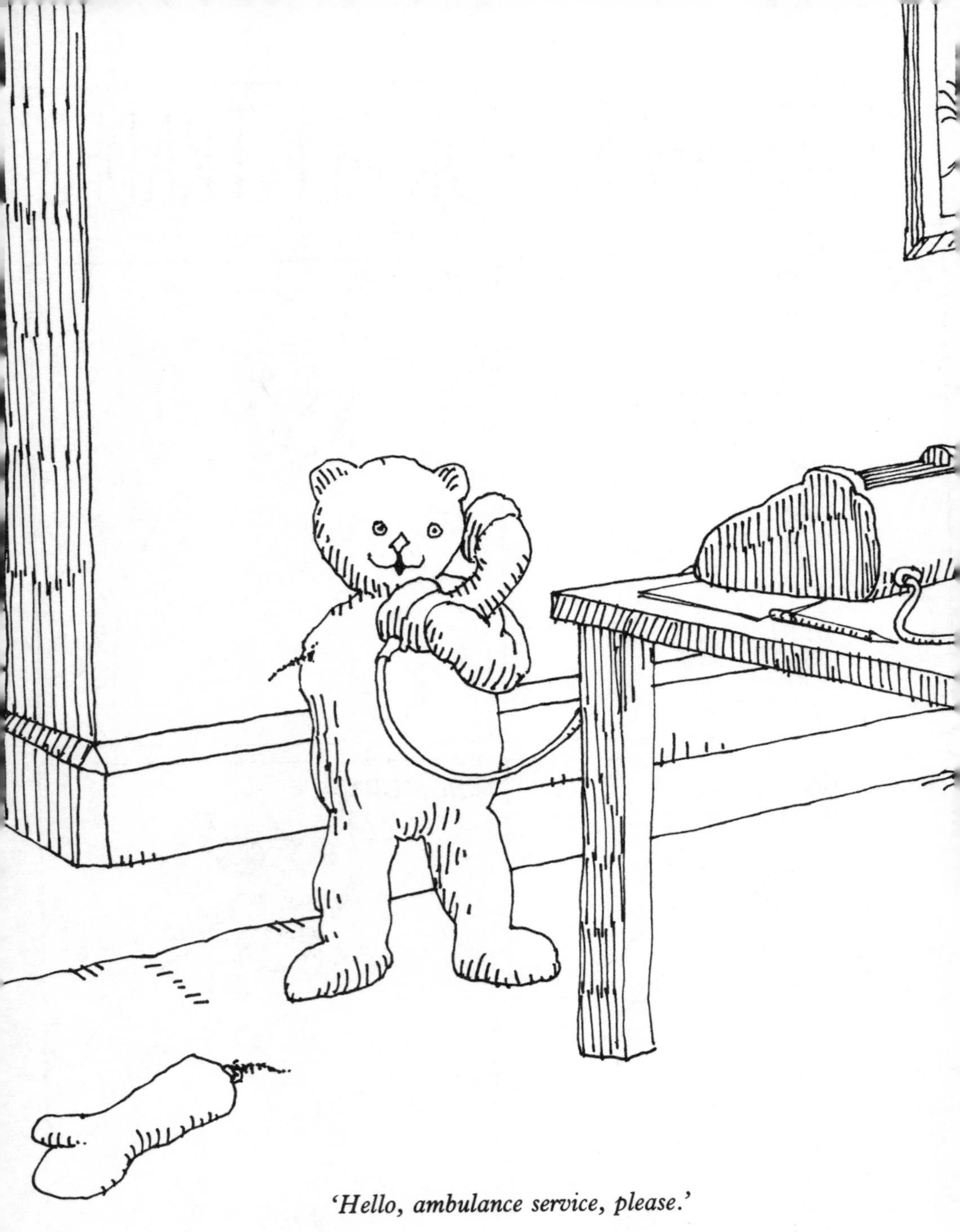

'Hello, ambulance service, please.'

The First Attempt

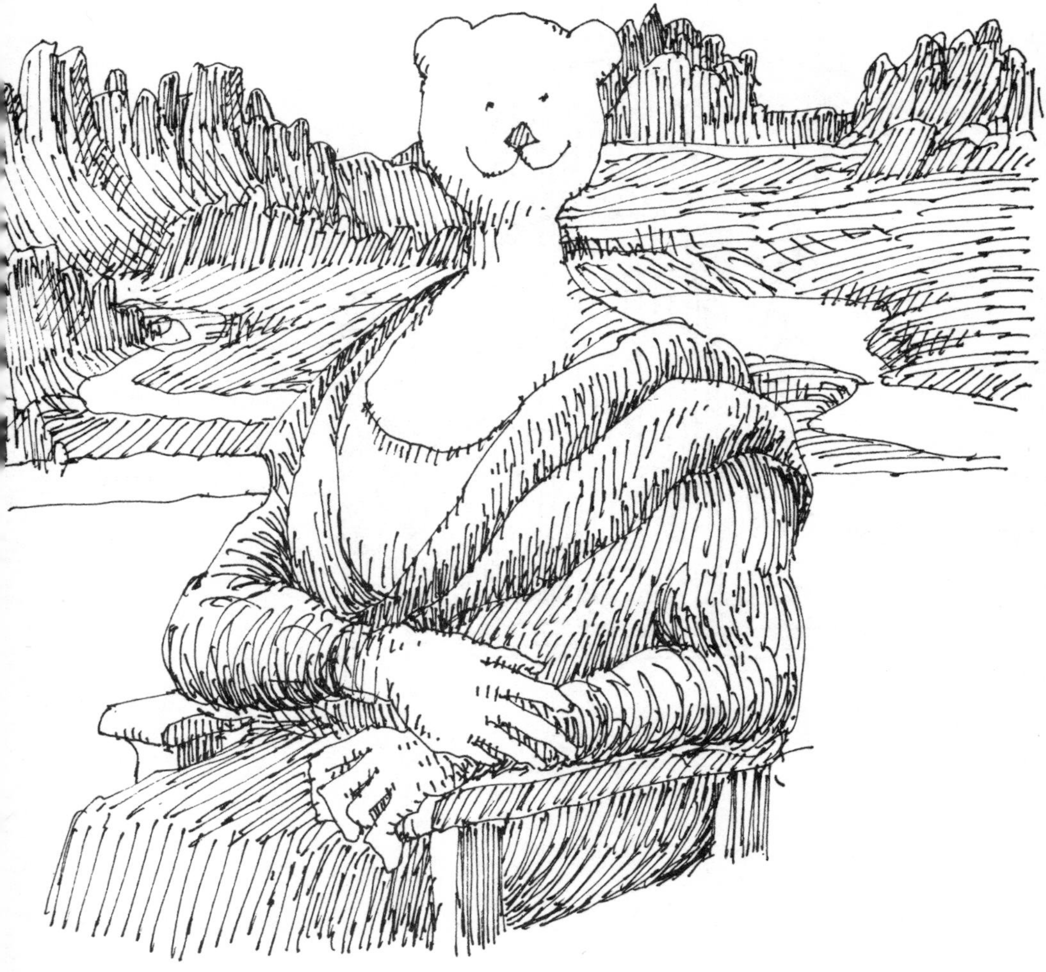

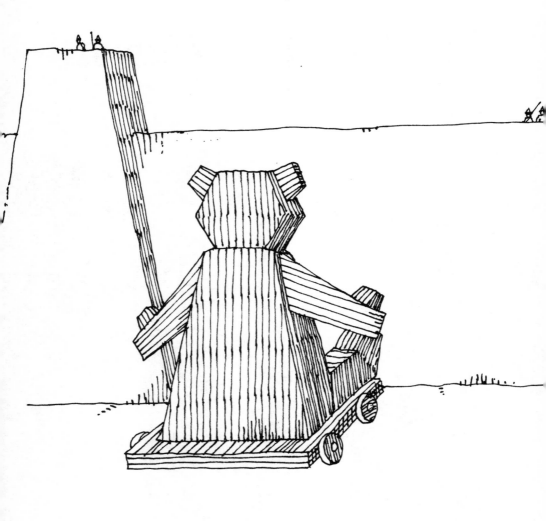

THE FIRST ATTEMPT

THE FIRST ATTEMPT

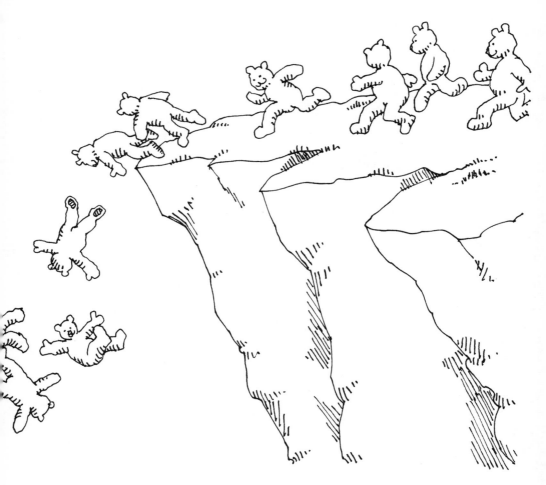

THE FIRST ATTEMPT

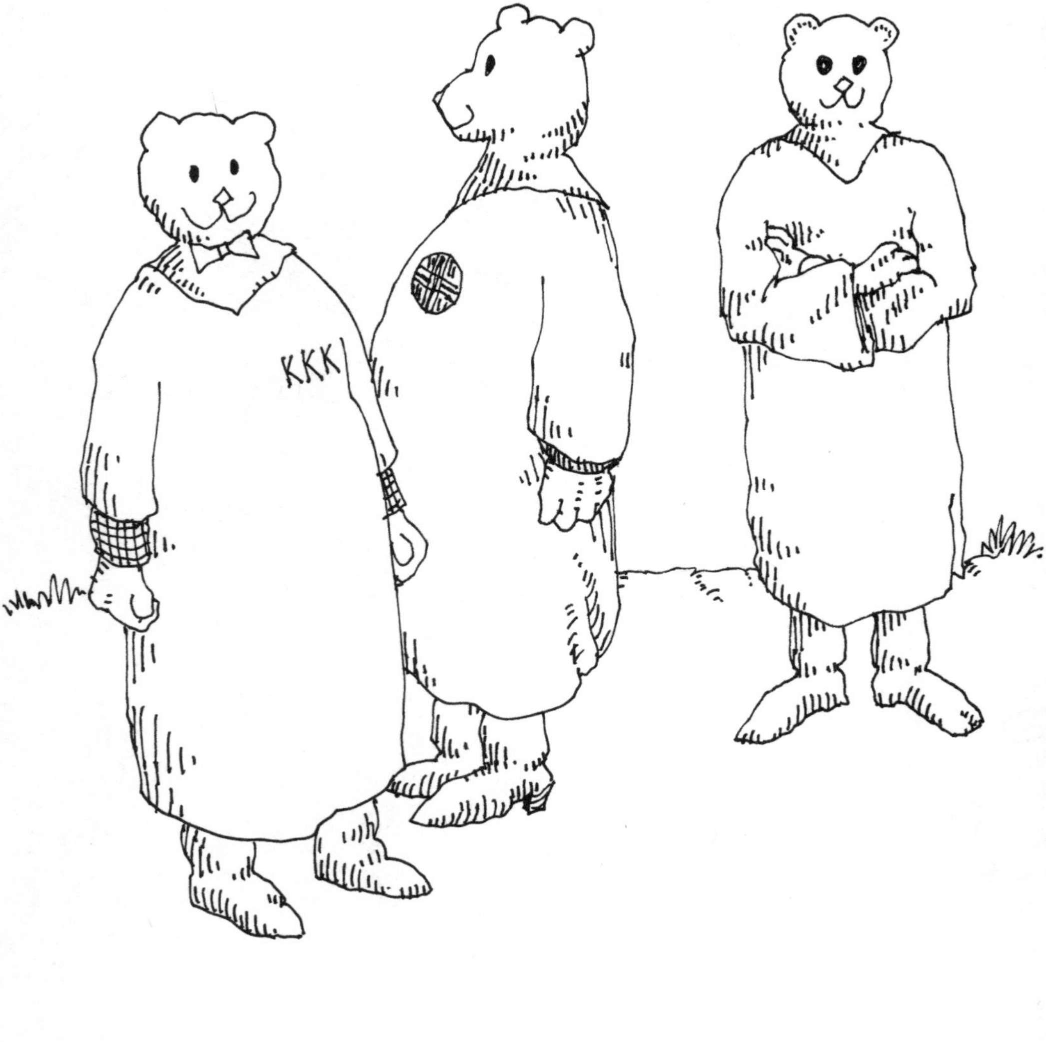
KKK

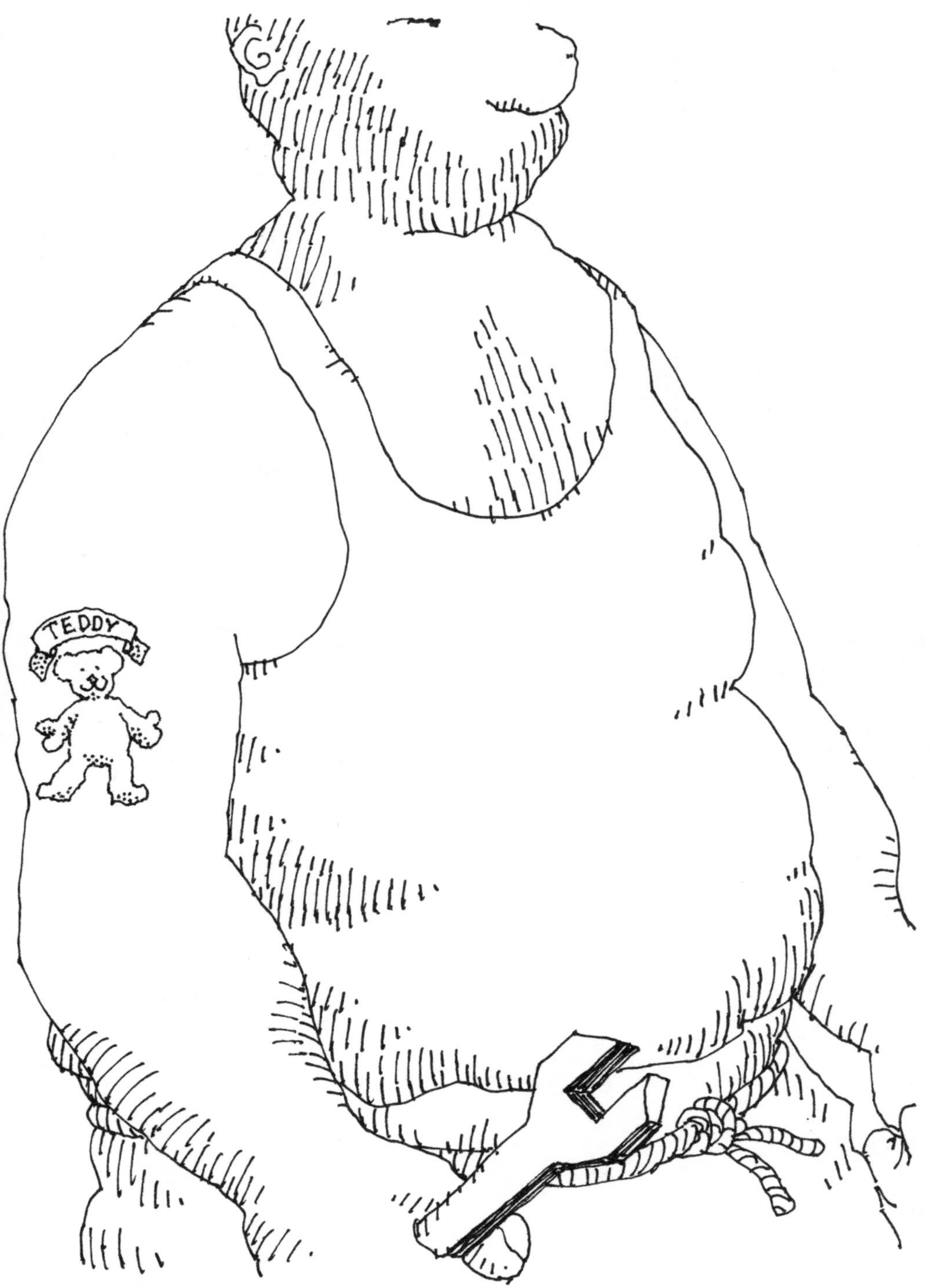
TEDDY

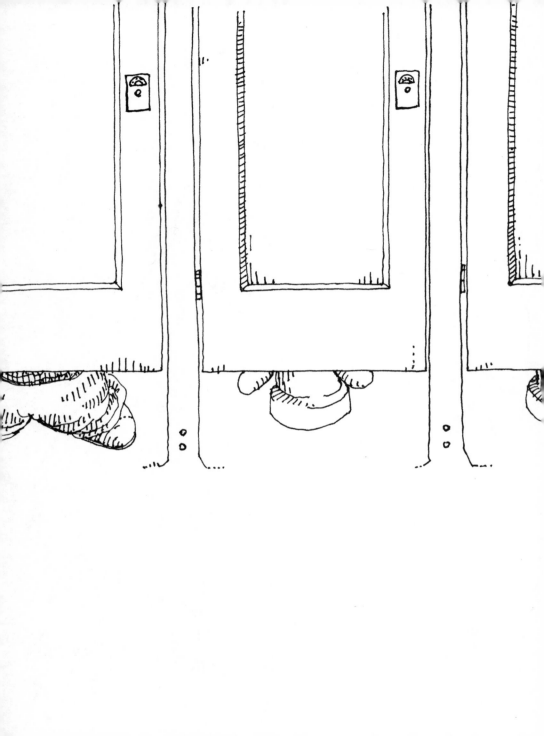

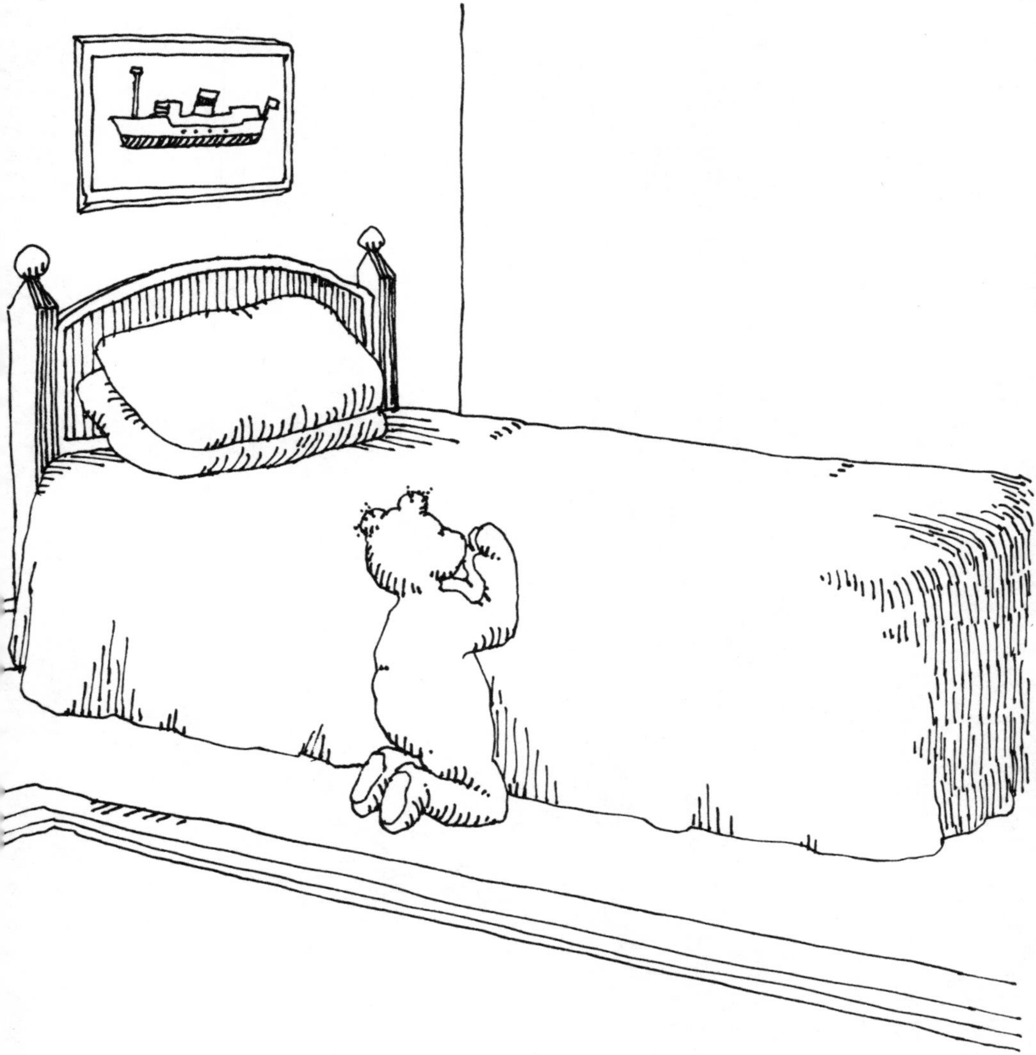

'. . . and please stop the little bastard chewing my ears.'

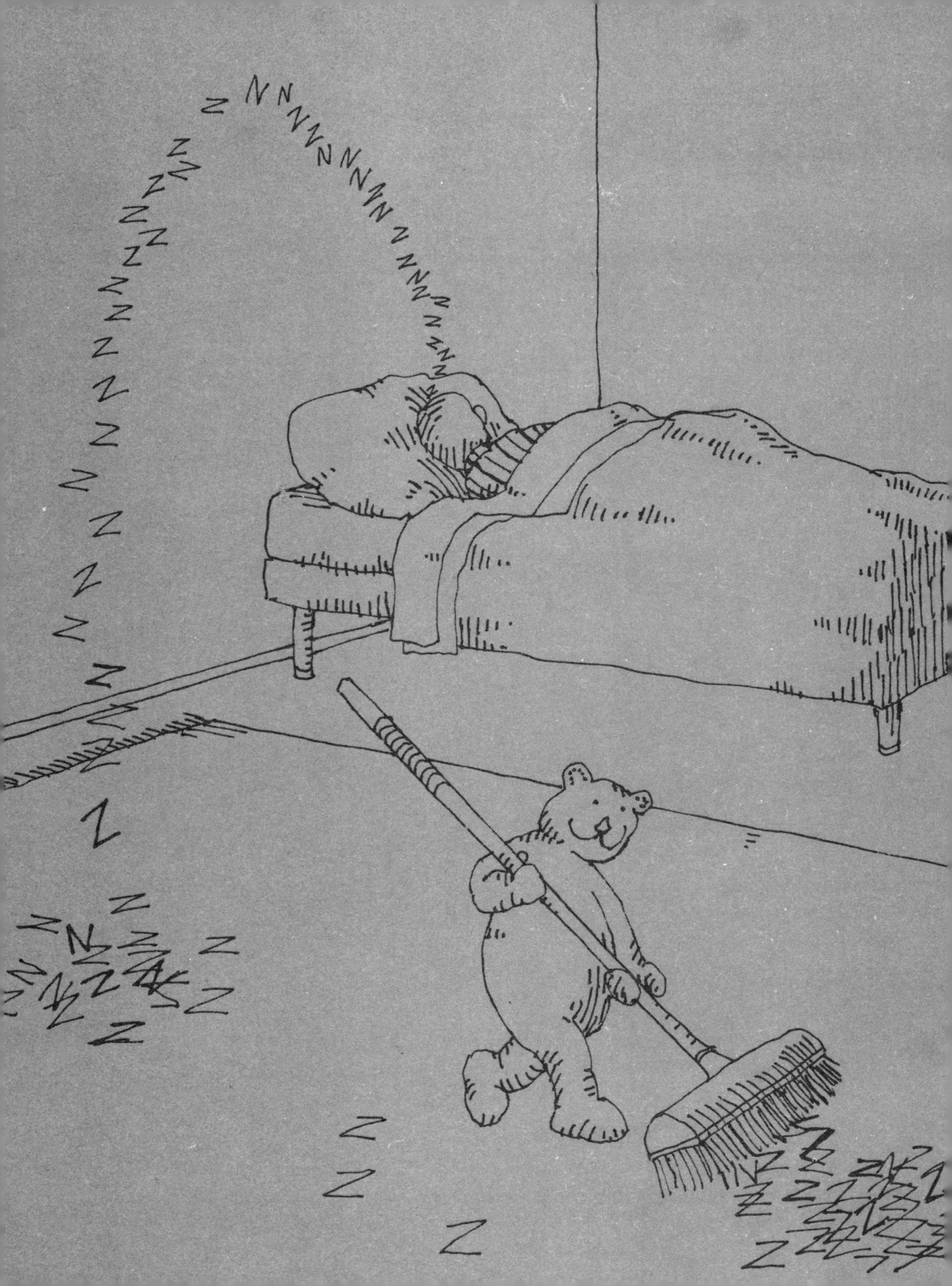

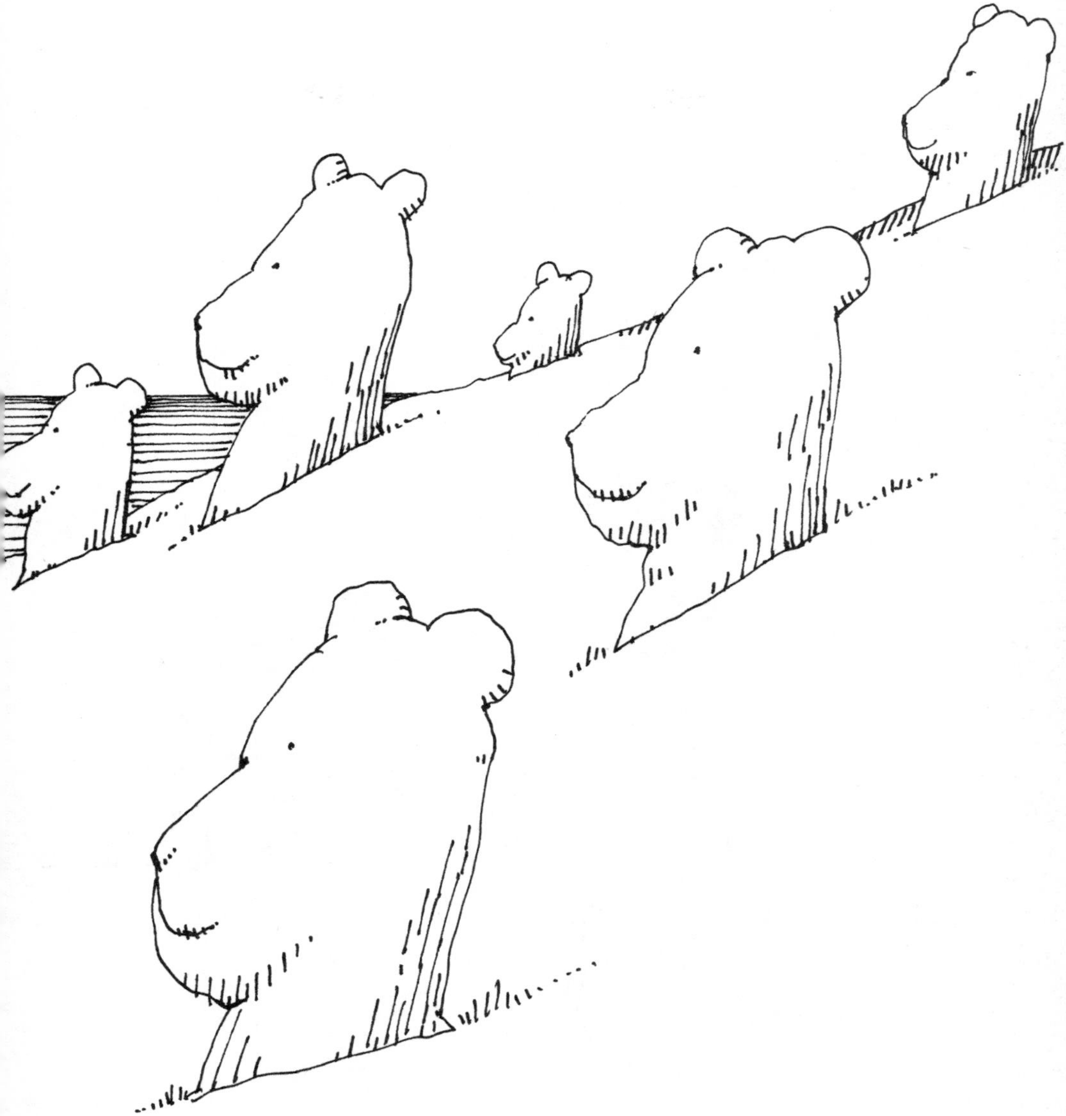

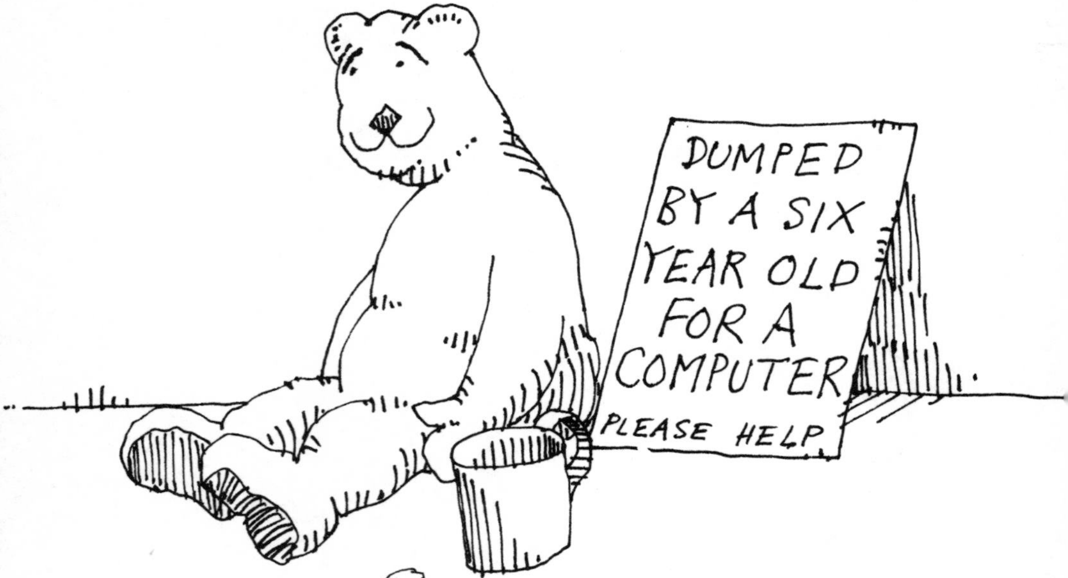
DUMPED
BY A SIX
YEAR OLD
FOR A
COMPUTER
PLEASE HELP

INSECURITY HITS WALL STREET

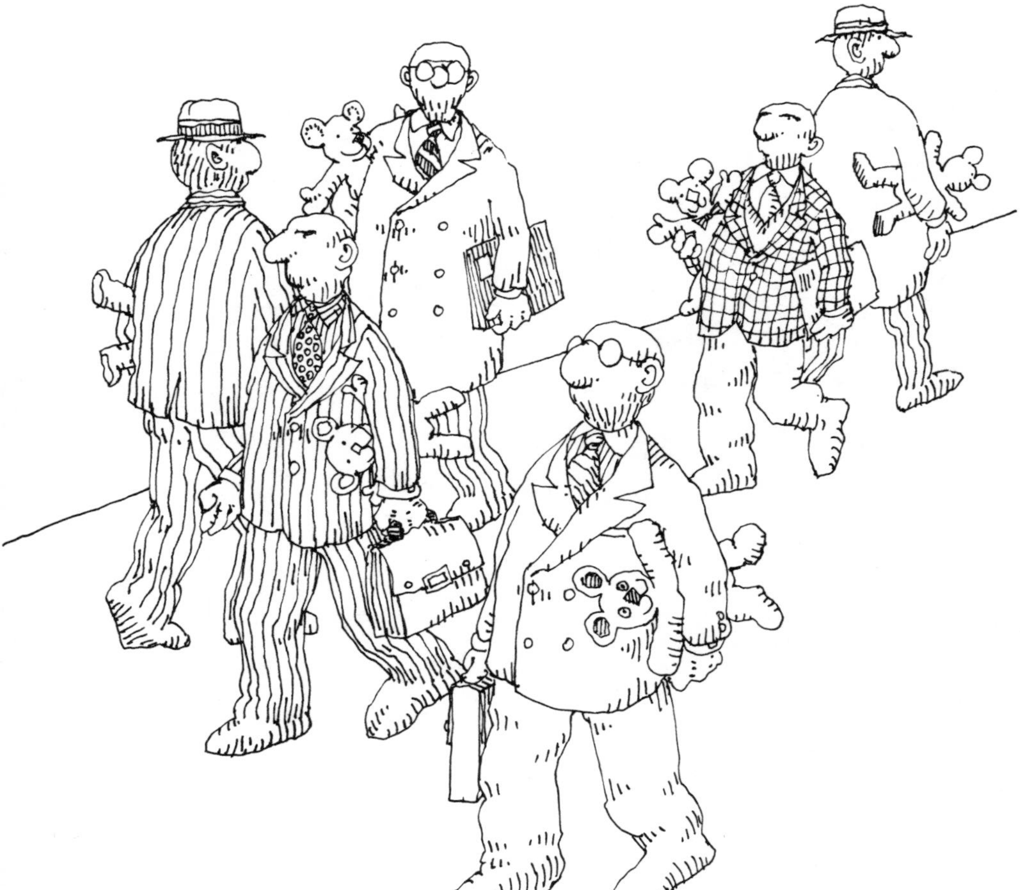

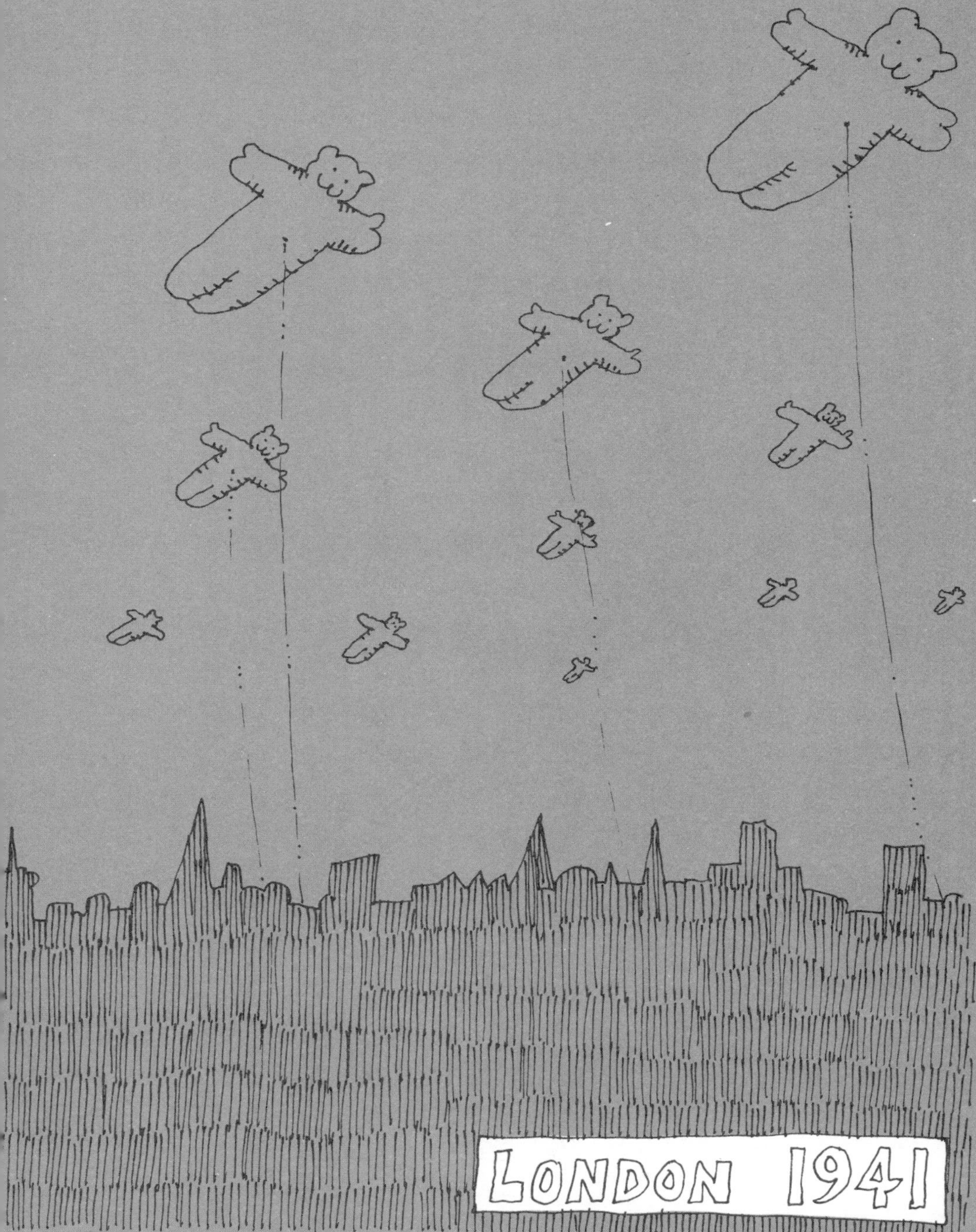
LONDON 1941

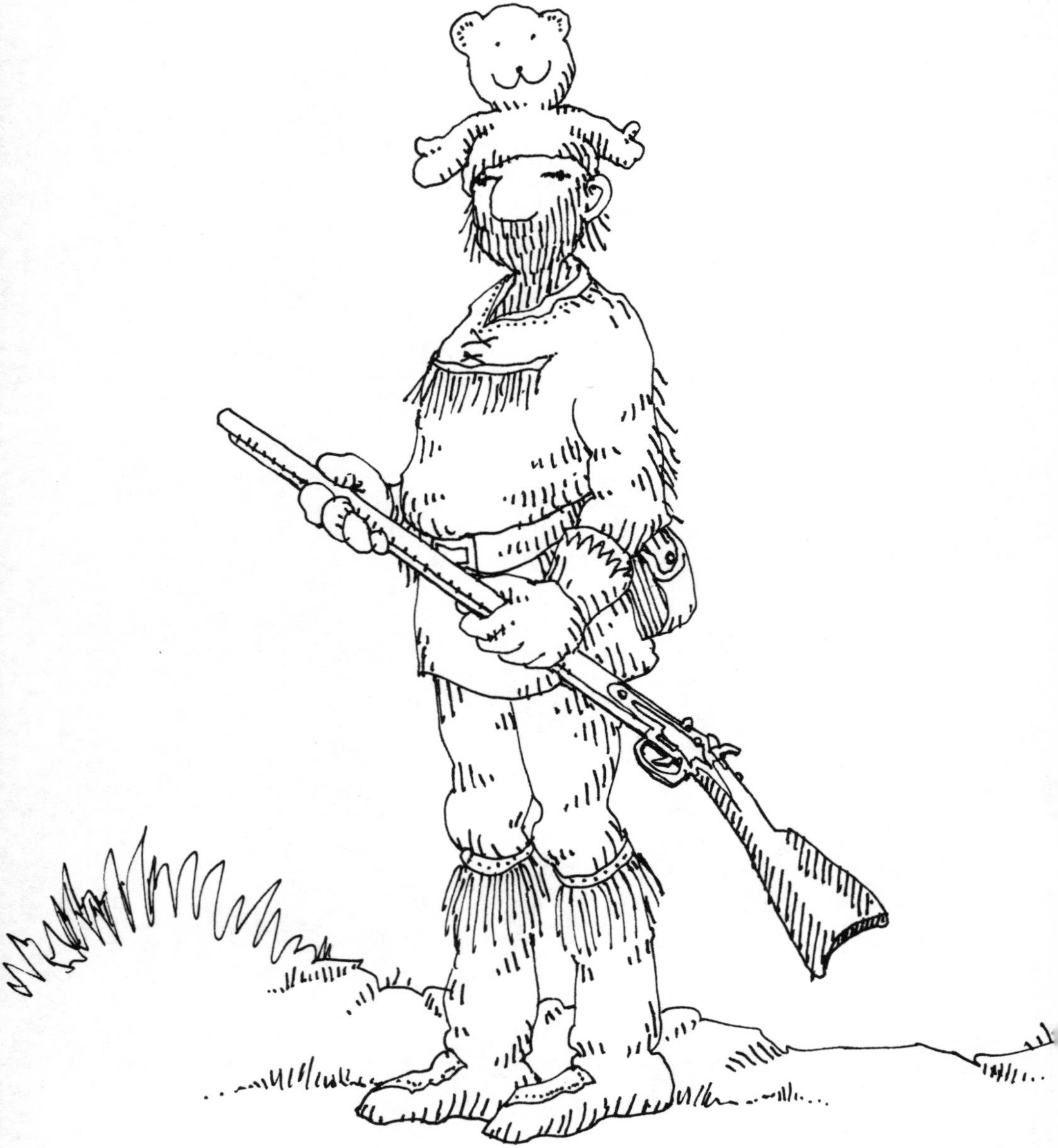

STUPIDITY No 1

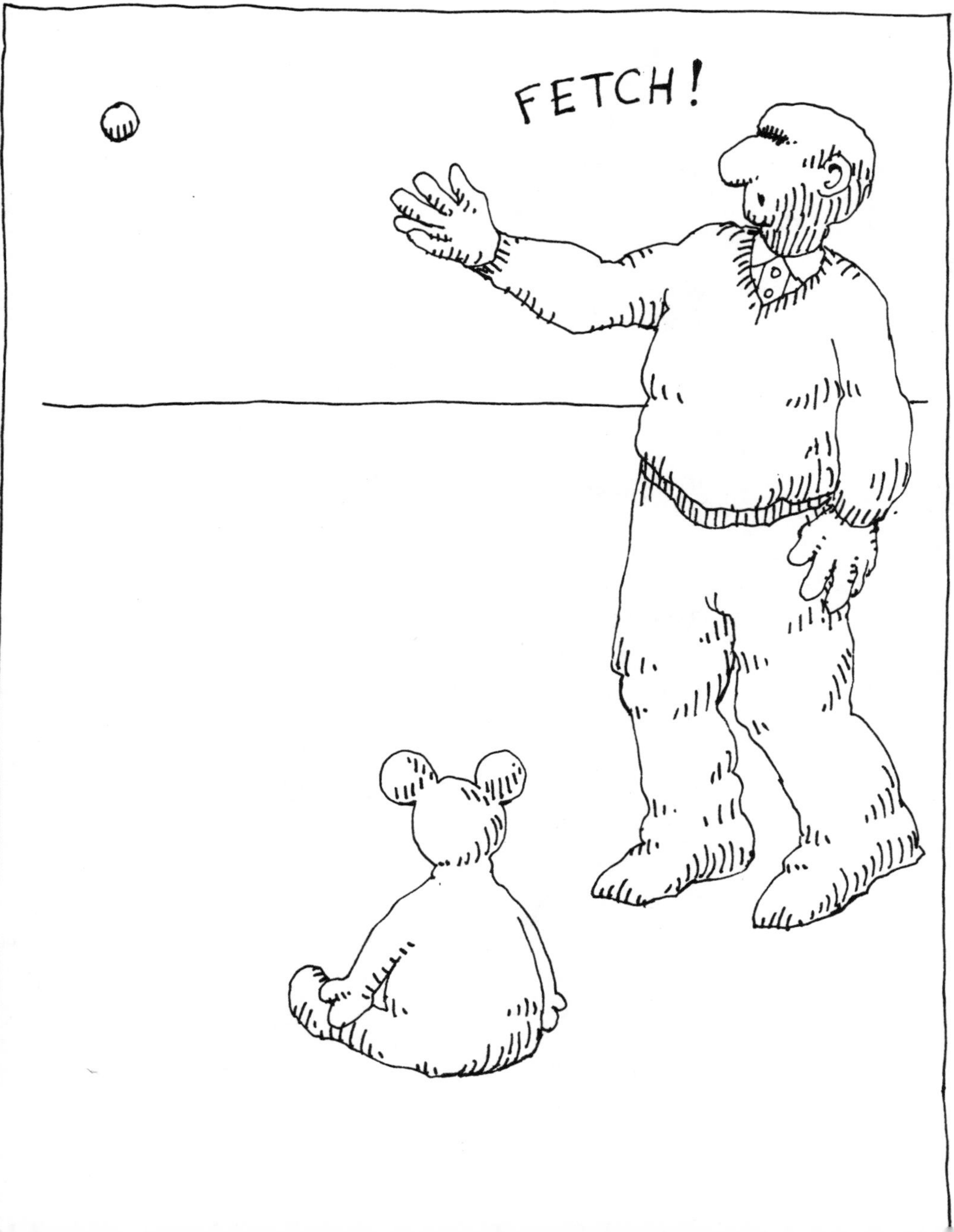
FETCH!

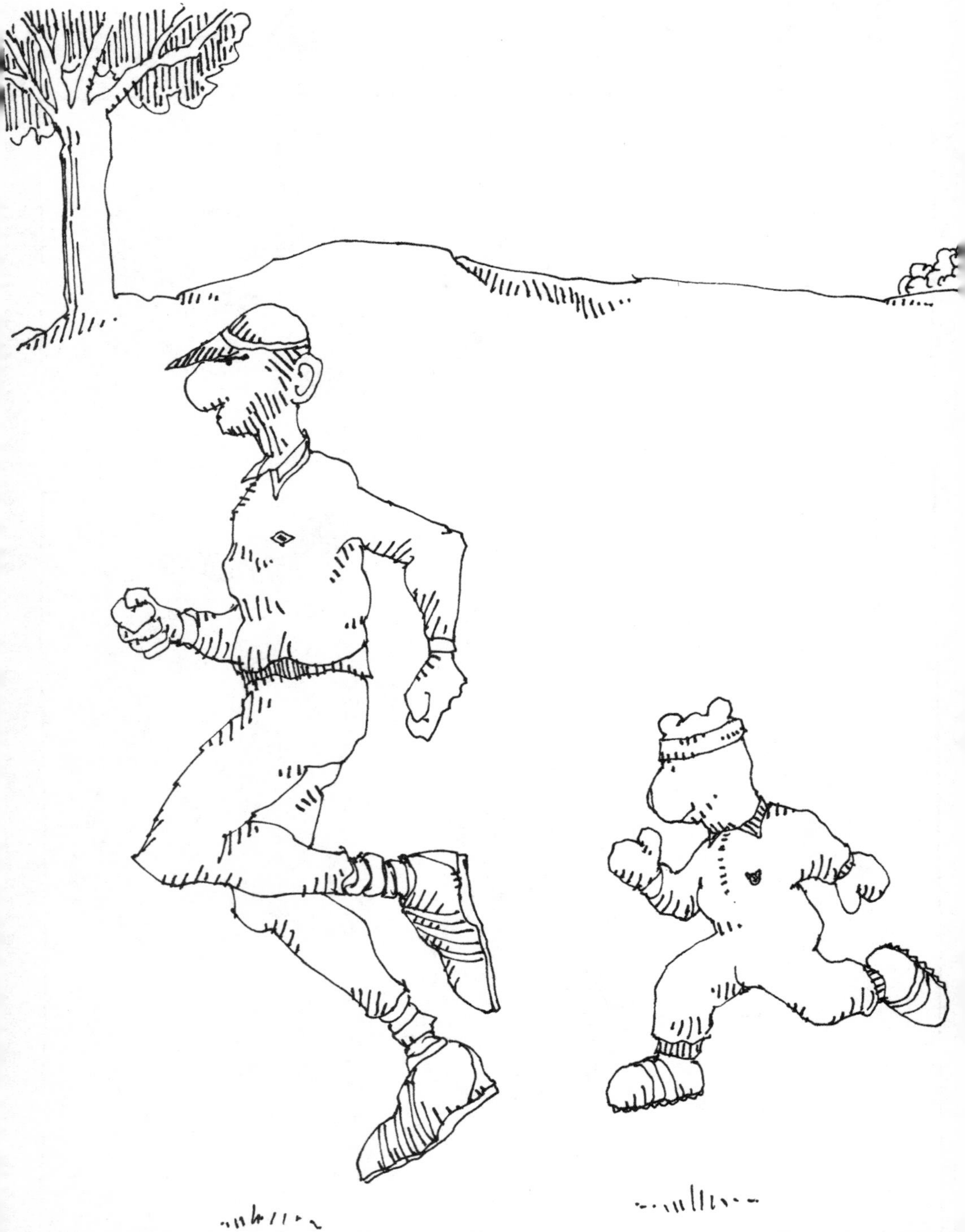

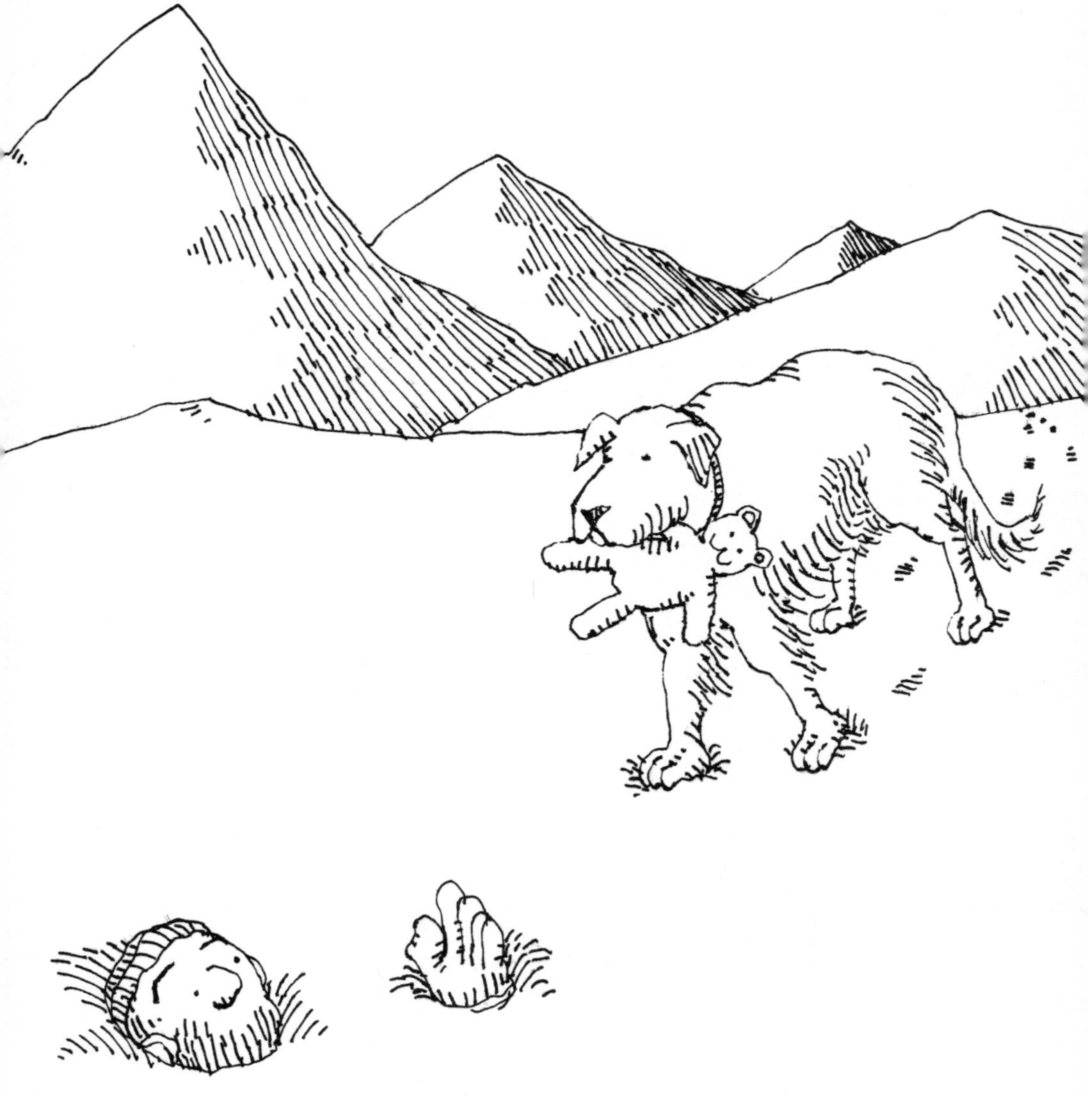

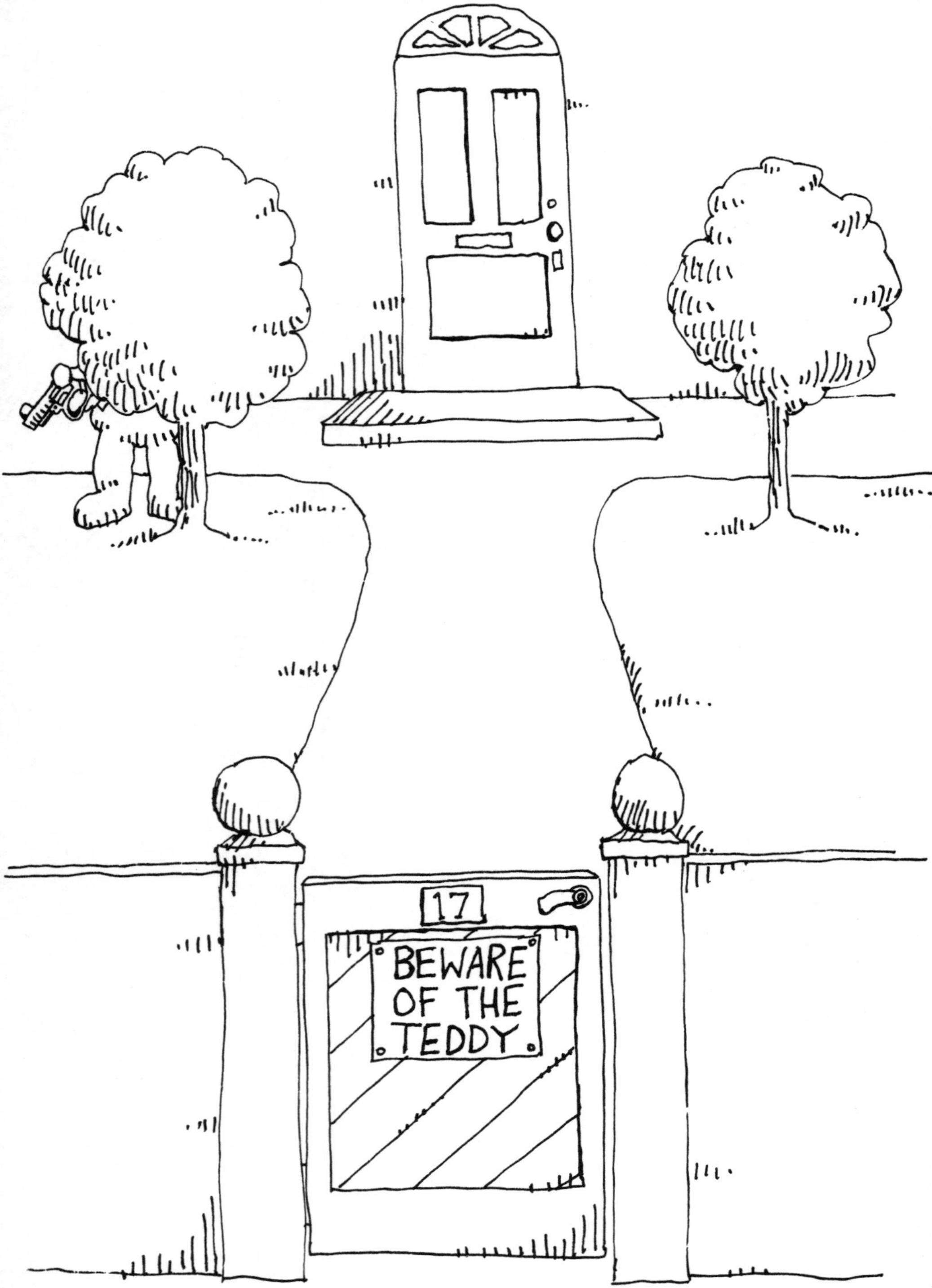
17
BEWARE OF THE TEDDY

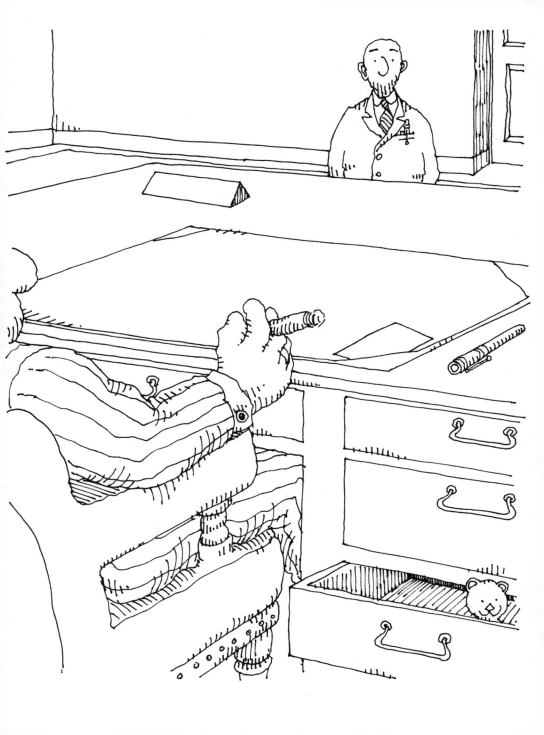

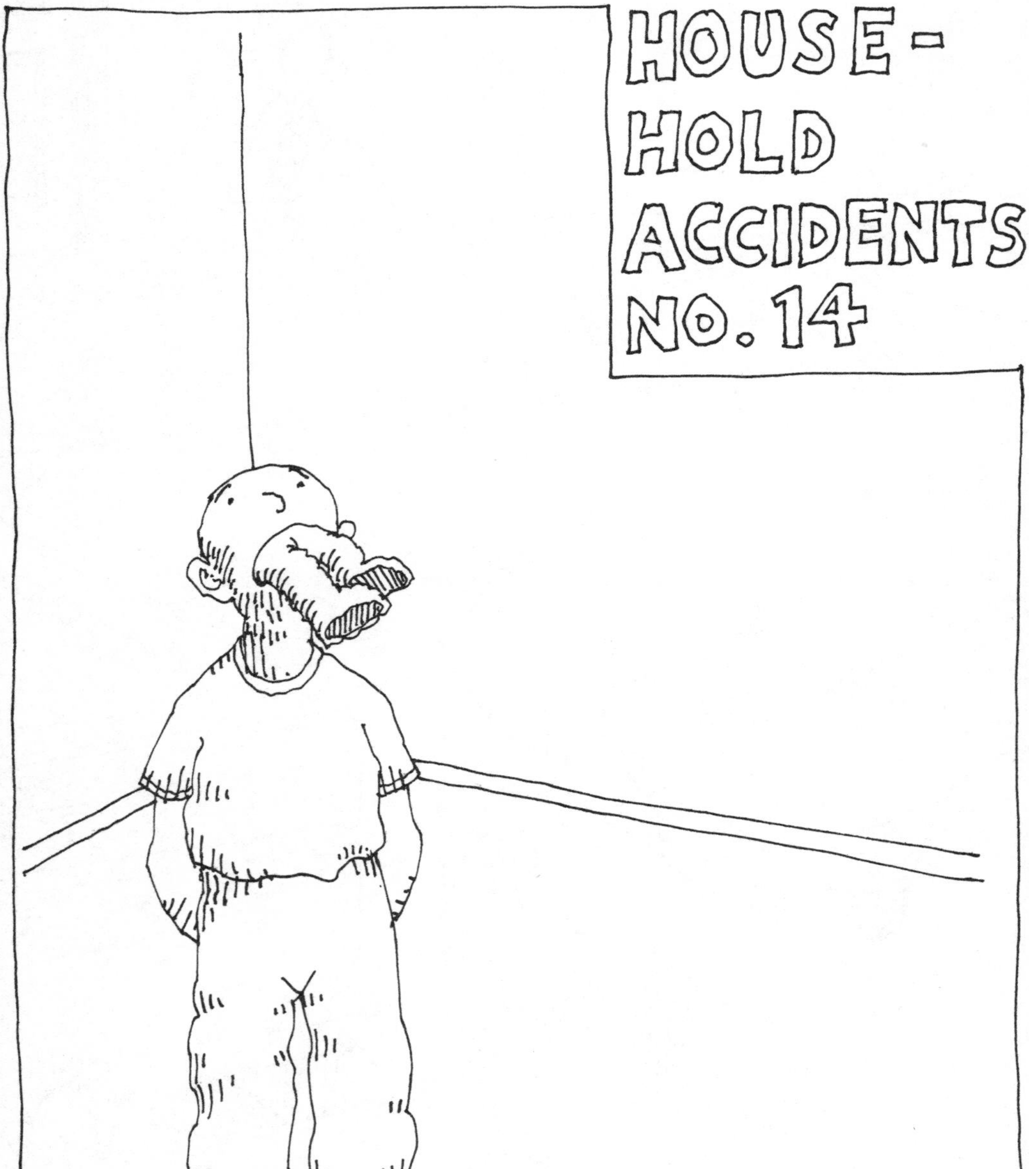
HOUSE-
HOLD
ACCIDENTS
NO. 14

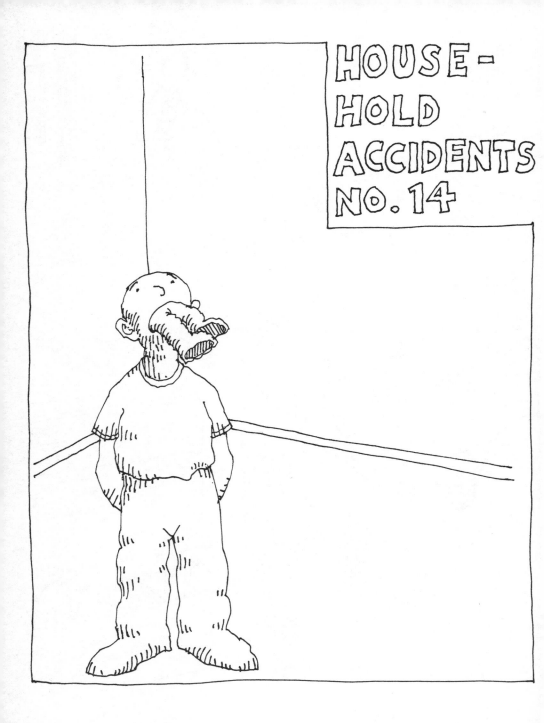

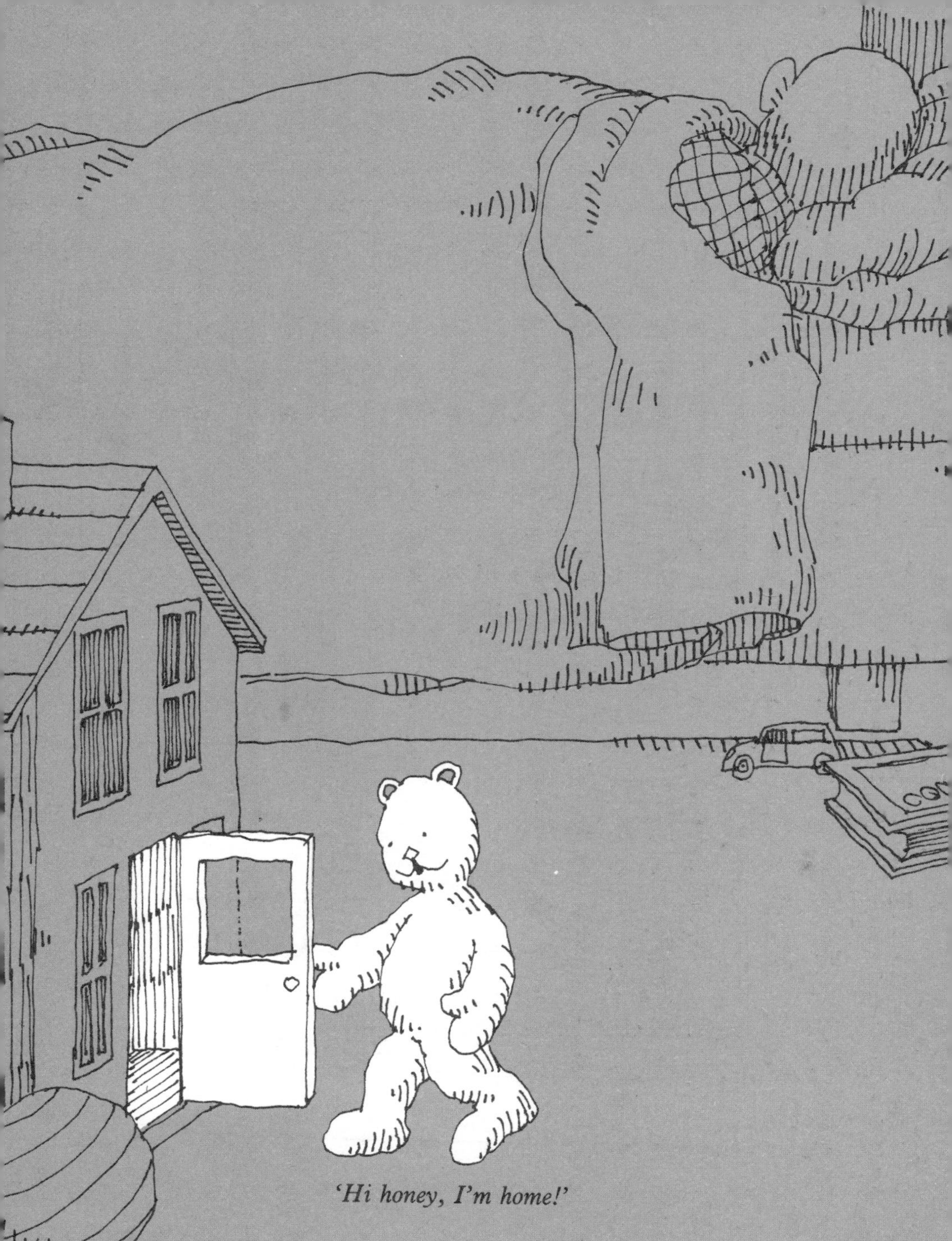

'Hi honey, I'm home!'

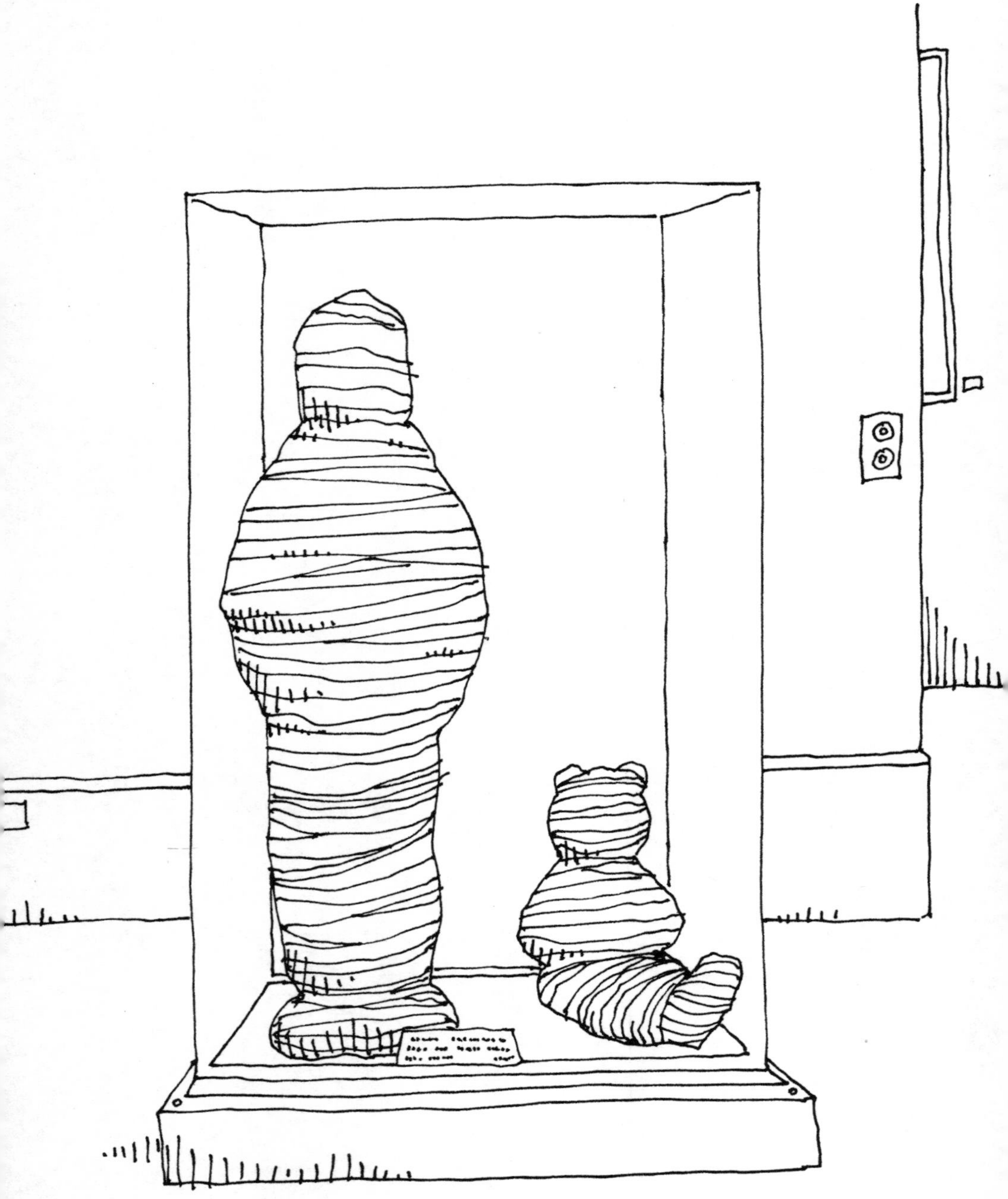

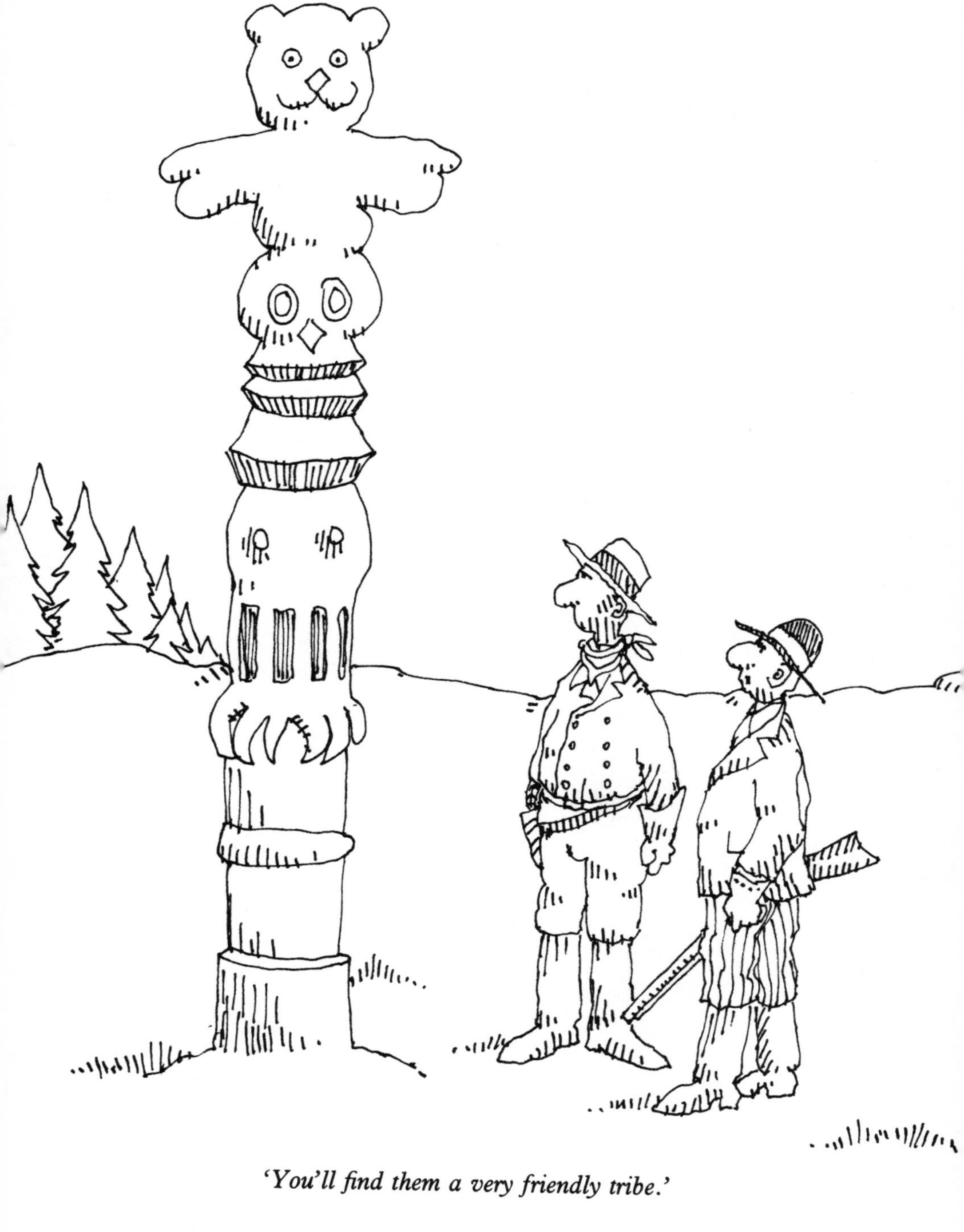

'You'll find them a very friendly tribe.'

TOUGH TERRITORY

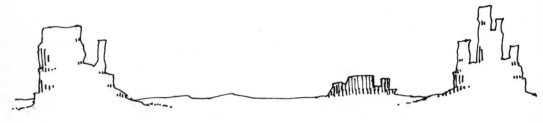

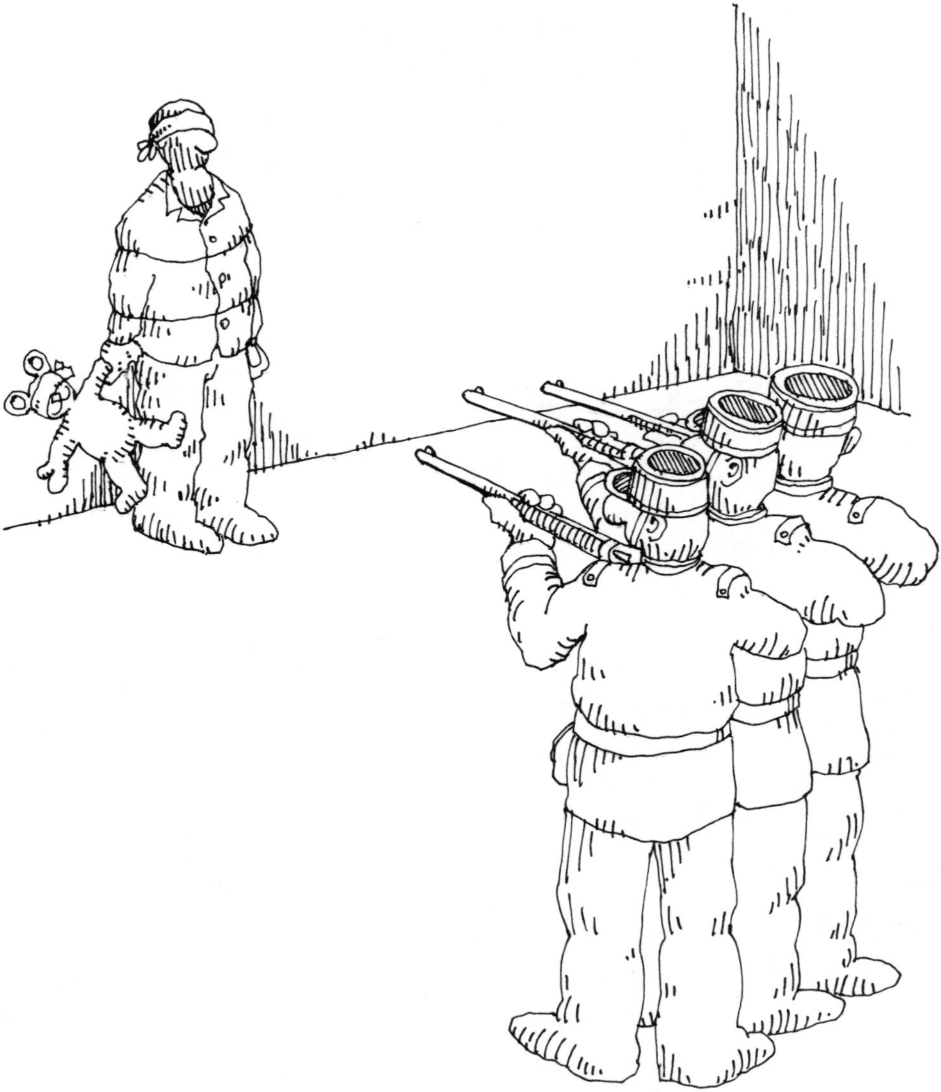

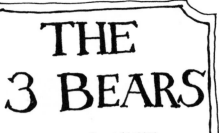

THE 3 BEARS

THE POCKET VERSION

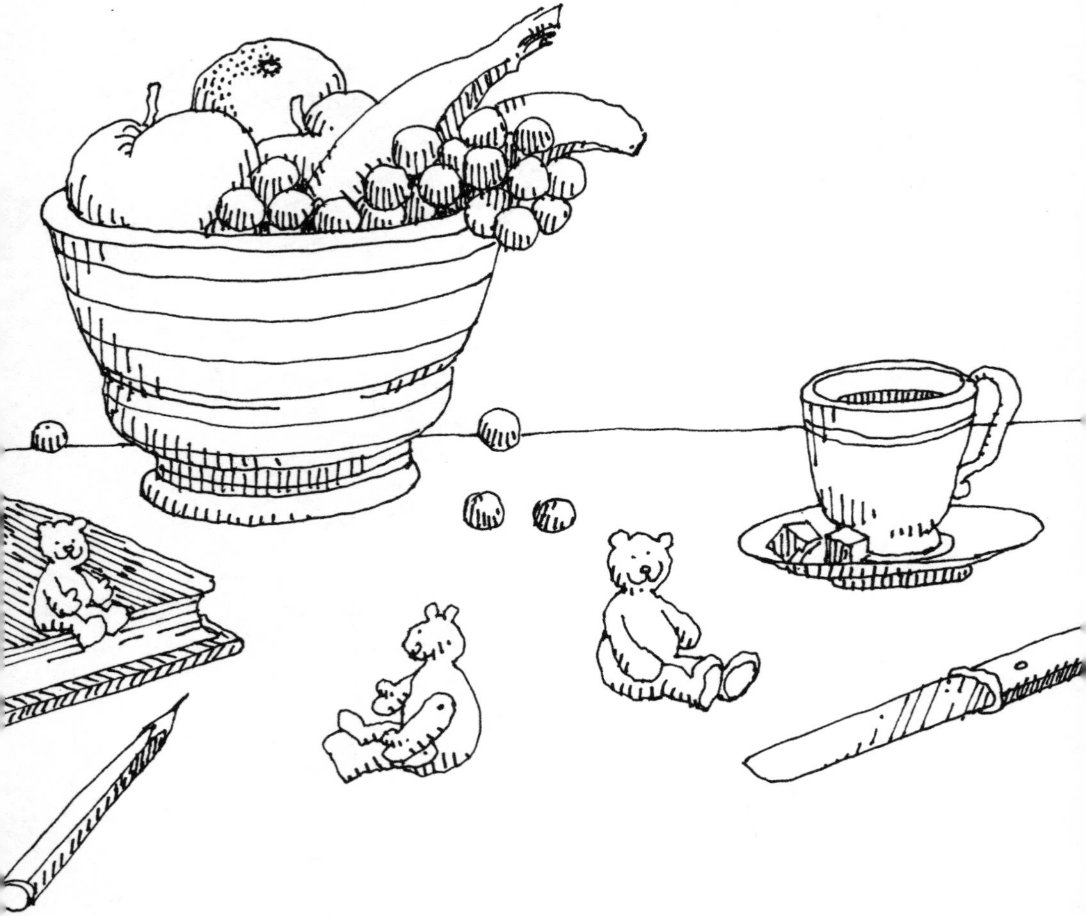

HOTEL HEARTLESS

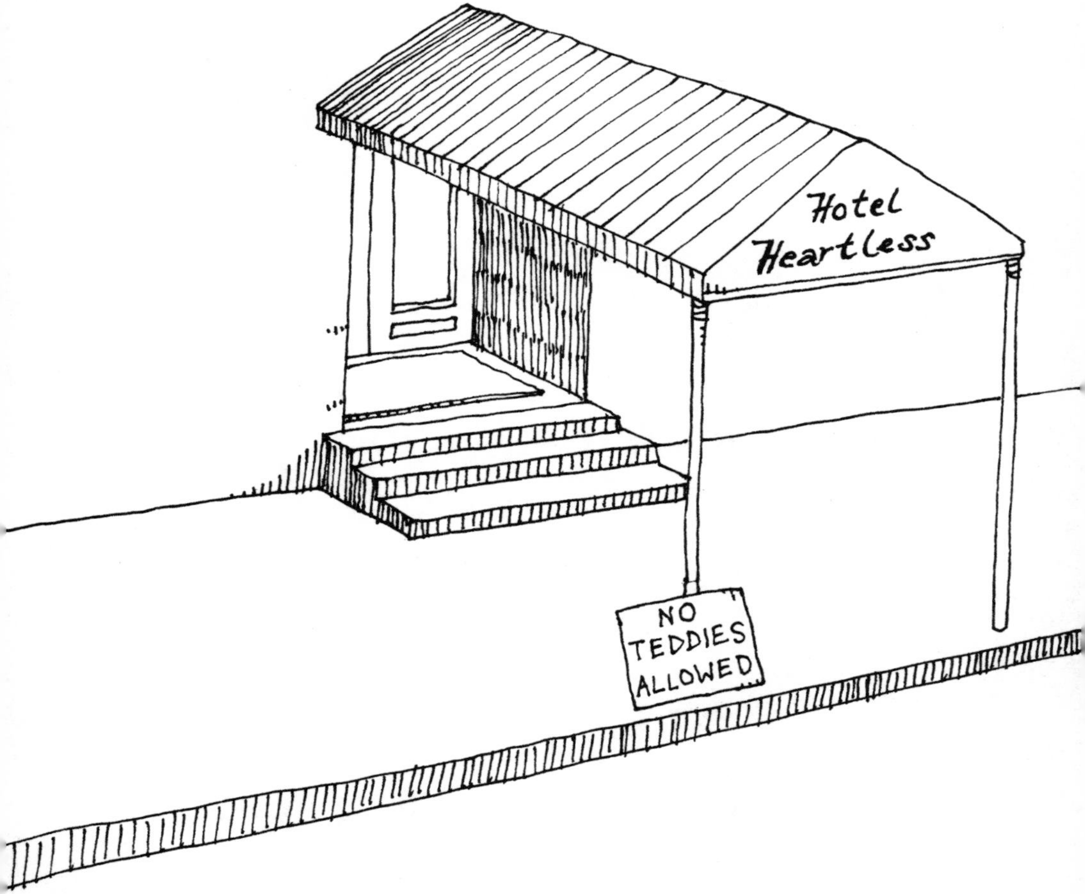
Hotel
Heartless
NO
TEDDIES
ALLOWED

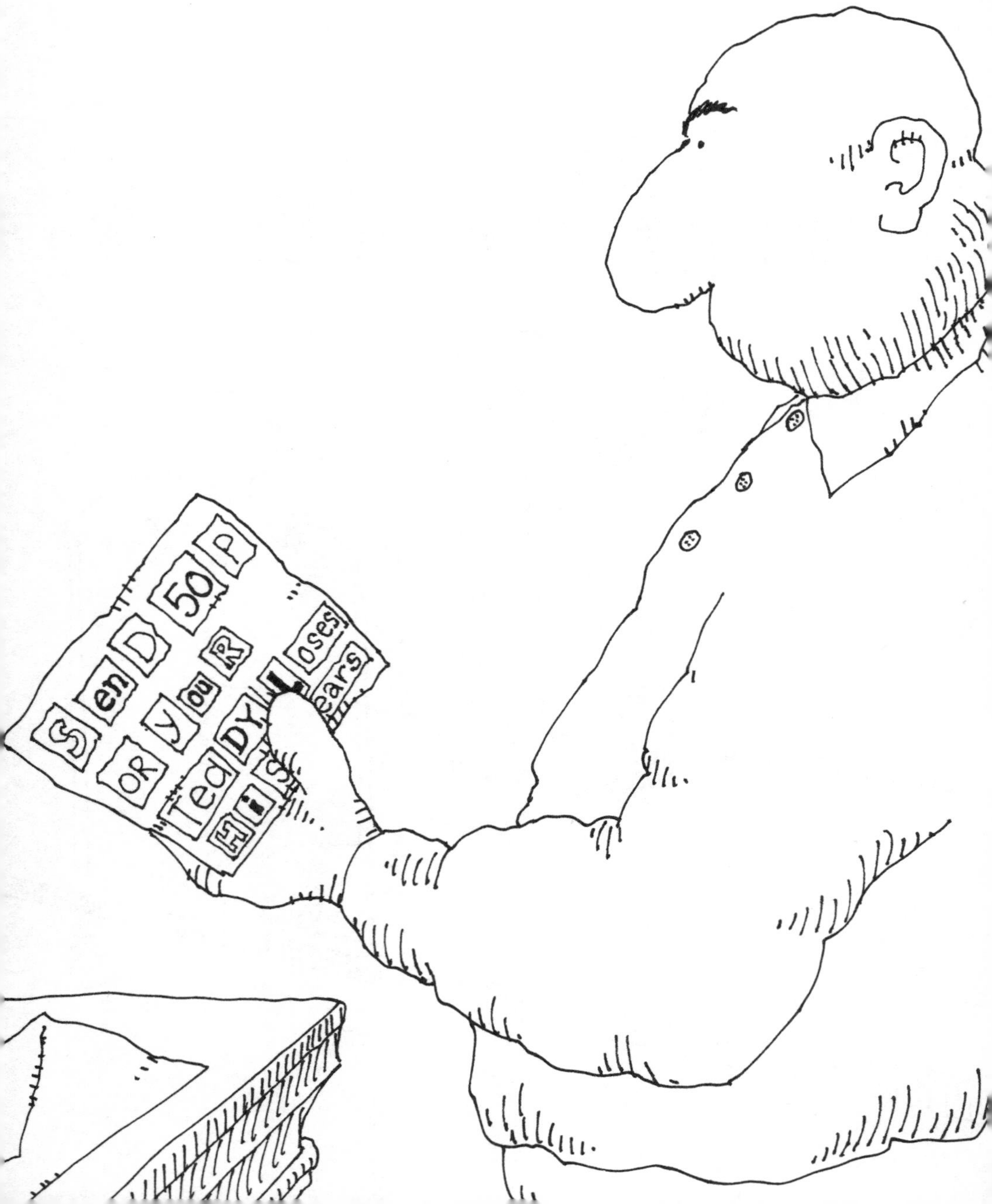

S en D 50 P
OR y ou R
Ted DY
oses
ears
Hi

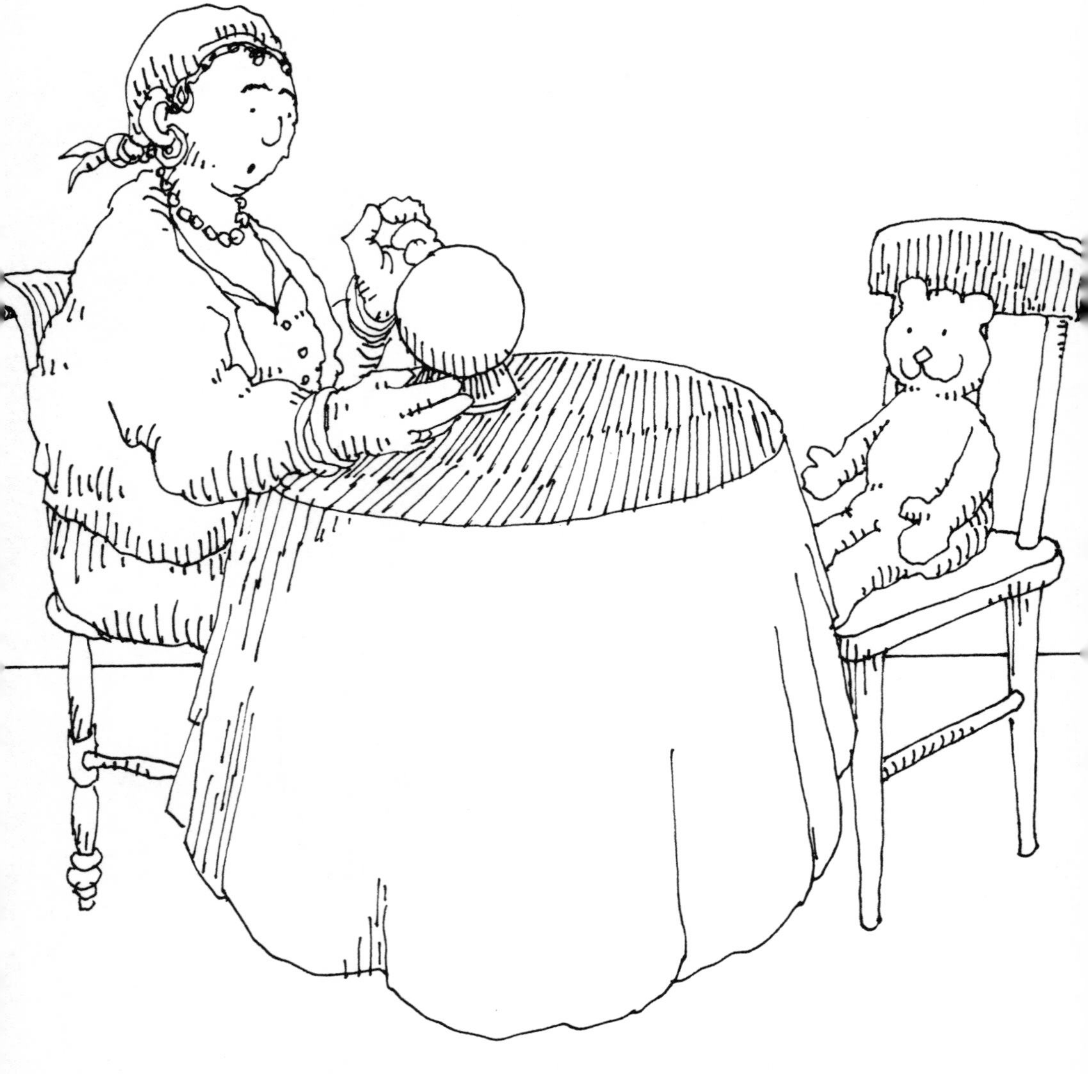

*'You will meet a small blonde who dribbles
and you will fall in love.'*

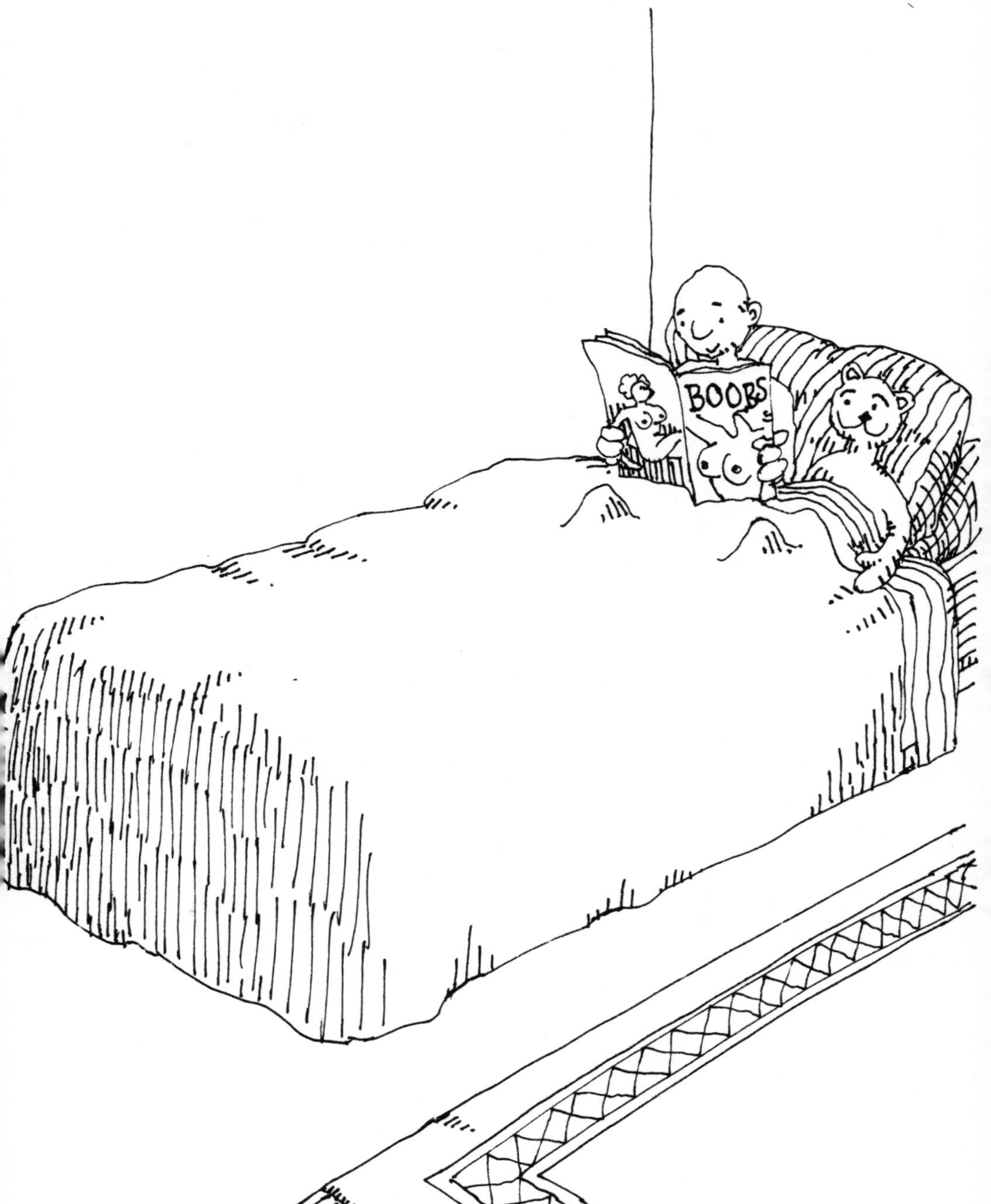
BOOBS

JOHN LOGIE ~~BEARD~~ BAIRD

THE INVENTOR OF THE ~~TEDDY~~ 'TELLY'

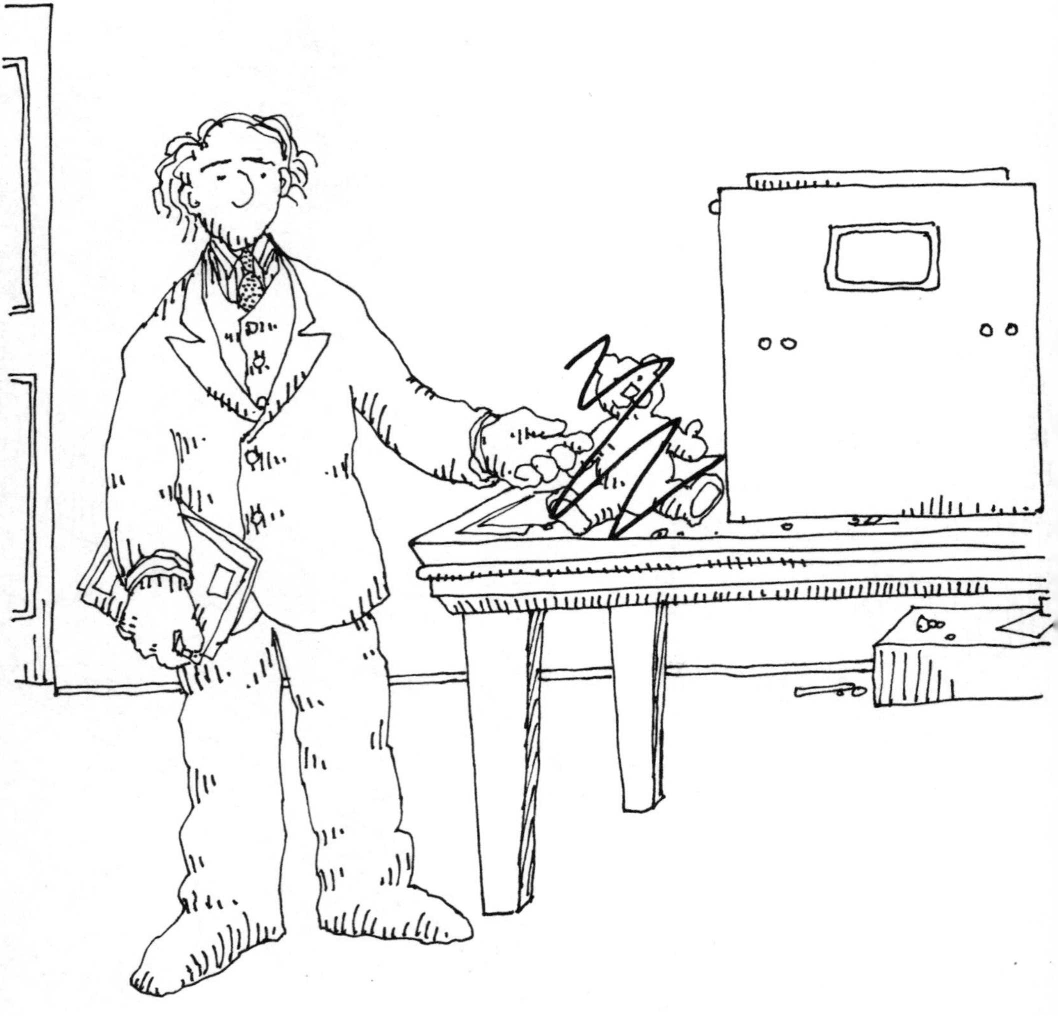

'*Don't fret Igor, it will do for the time being.*'

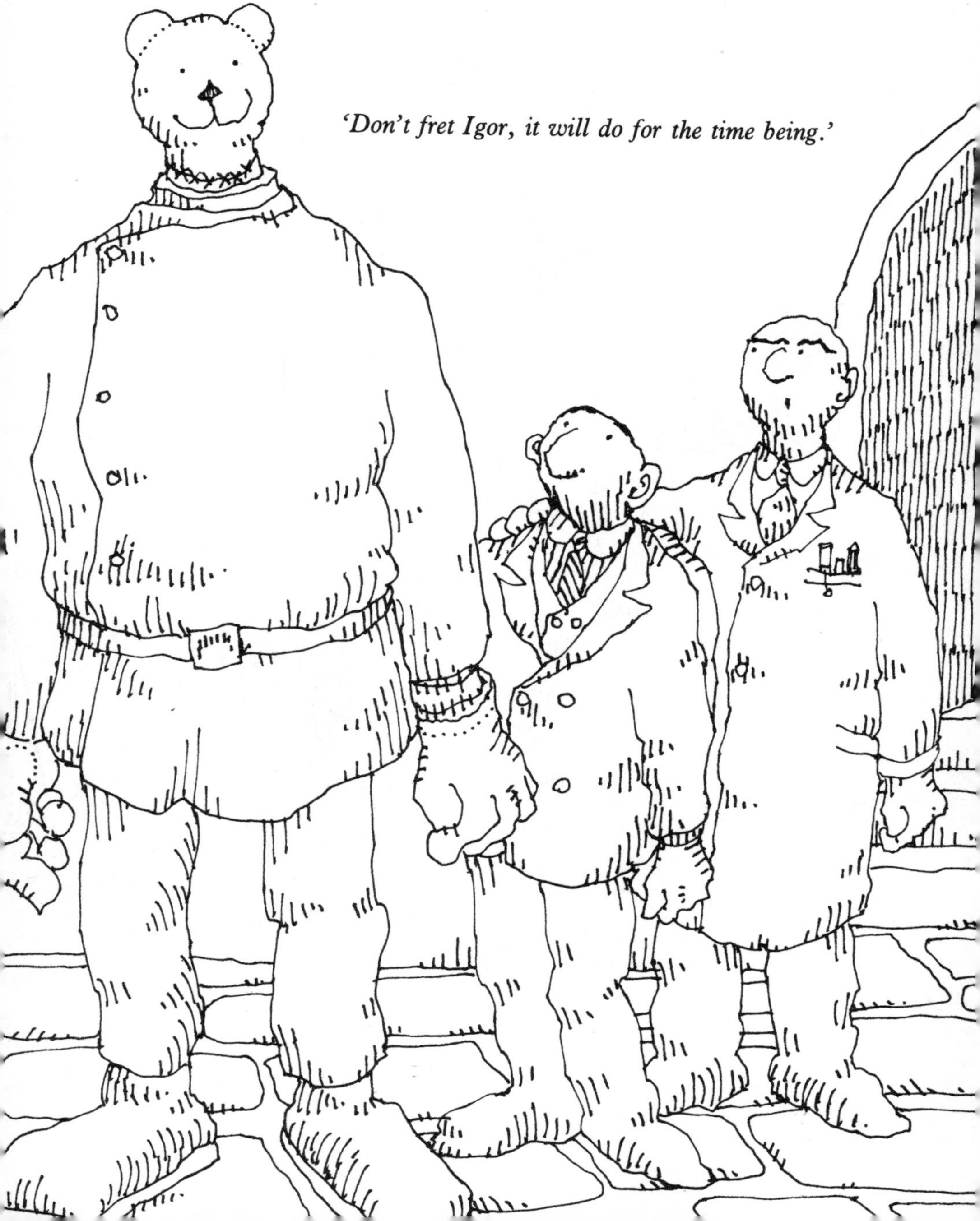

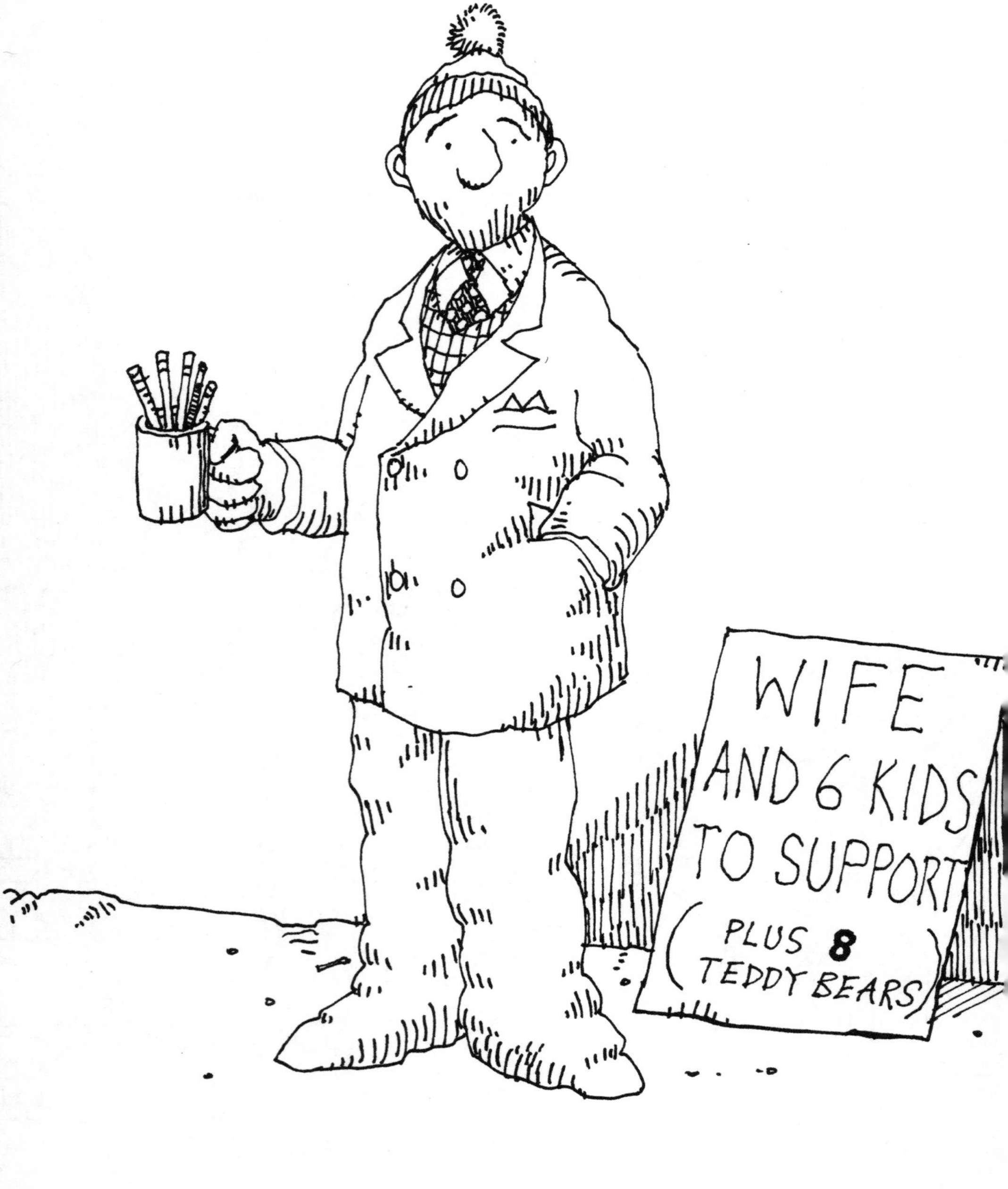
WIFE
AND 6 KIDS
TO SUPPORT
(PLUS 8
TEDDY BEARS)

'. . . and finally thirty-eight million Teddybears!'

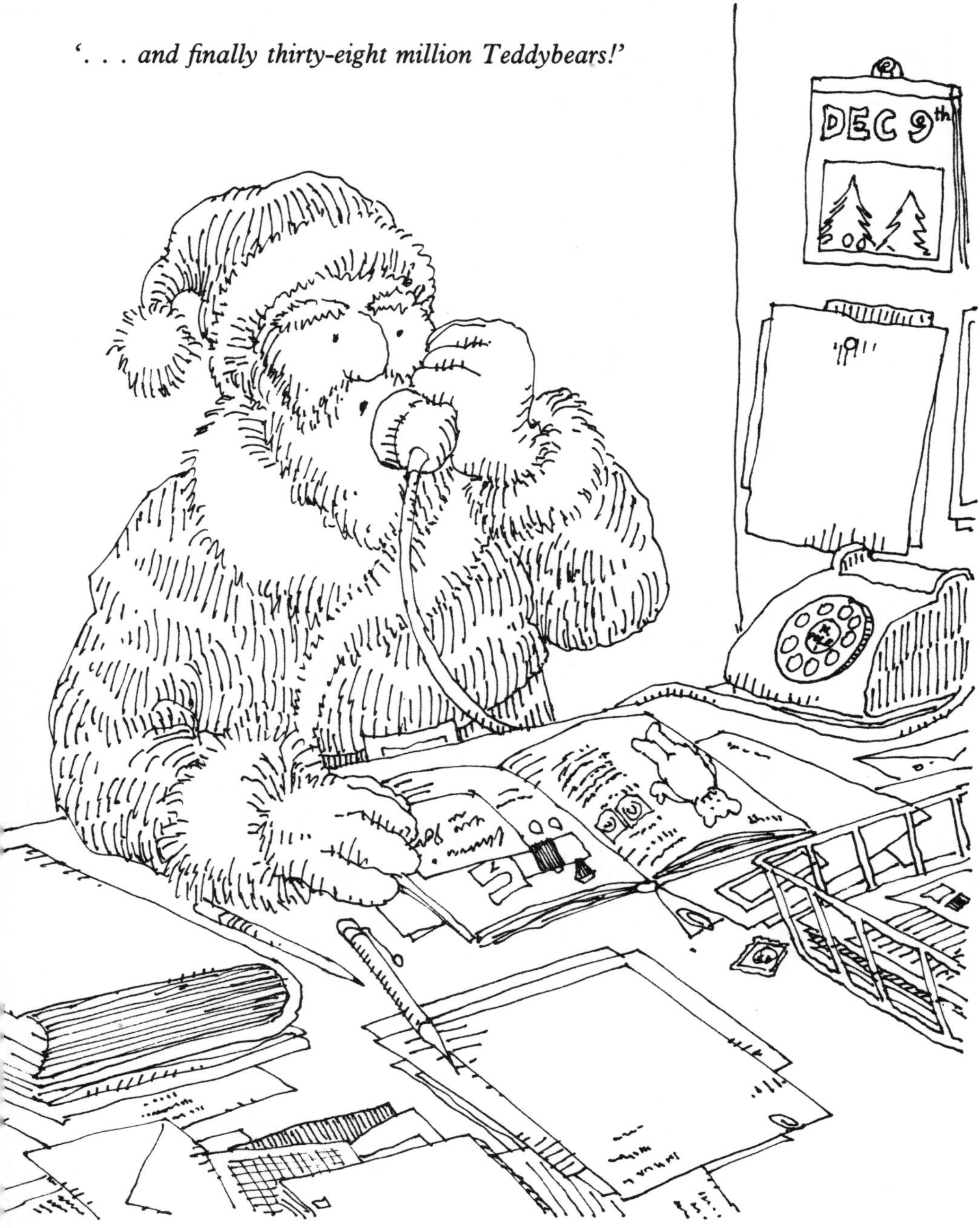
DEC 9th
9

THE TEDDY TEST

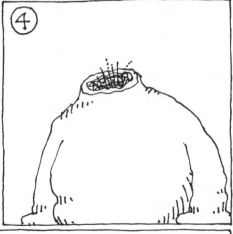

○ LORD NELSON   ○ VINCENT VAN GOGH
○ CHARLES MANSON ○ RICHARD III

match each Teddy with their very famous owners.

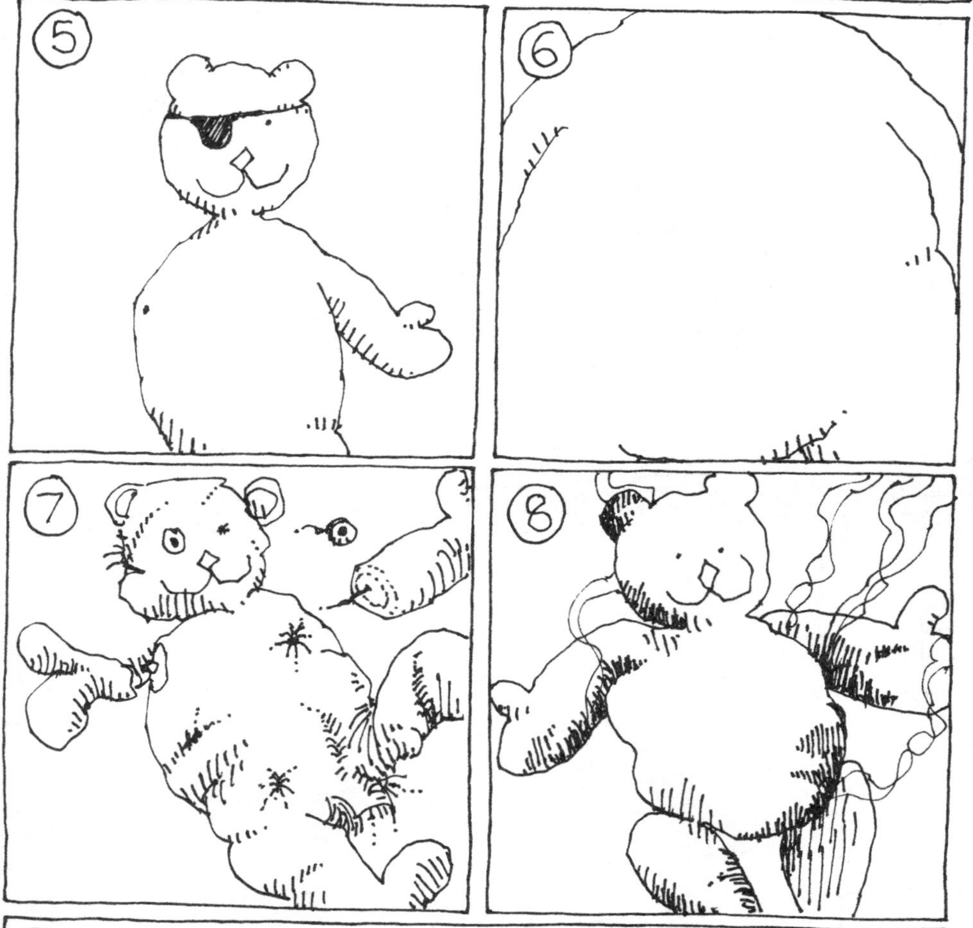
5
6
7
8

- ◯ ORSON WELLES
- ◯ CHARLES I
- ◯ JOAN OF ARC
- ◯ CYRANO DE BERGERAC

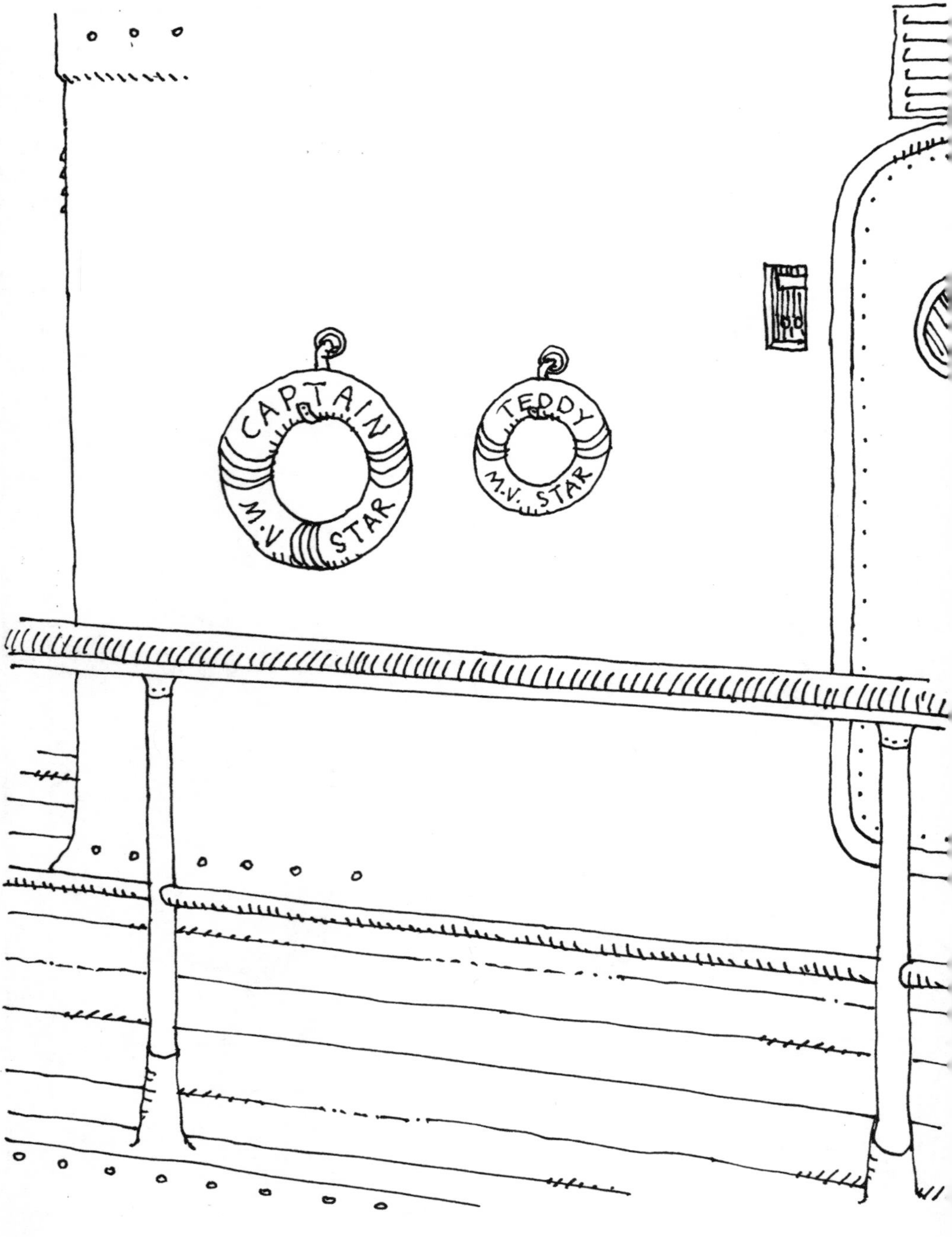
CAPTAIN
M.V. STAR
TEDDY
M.V. STAR

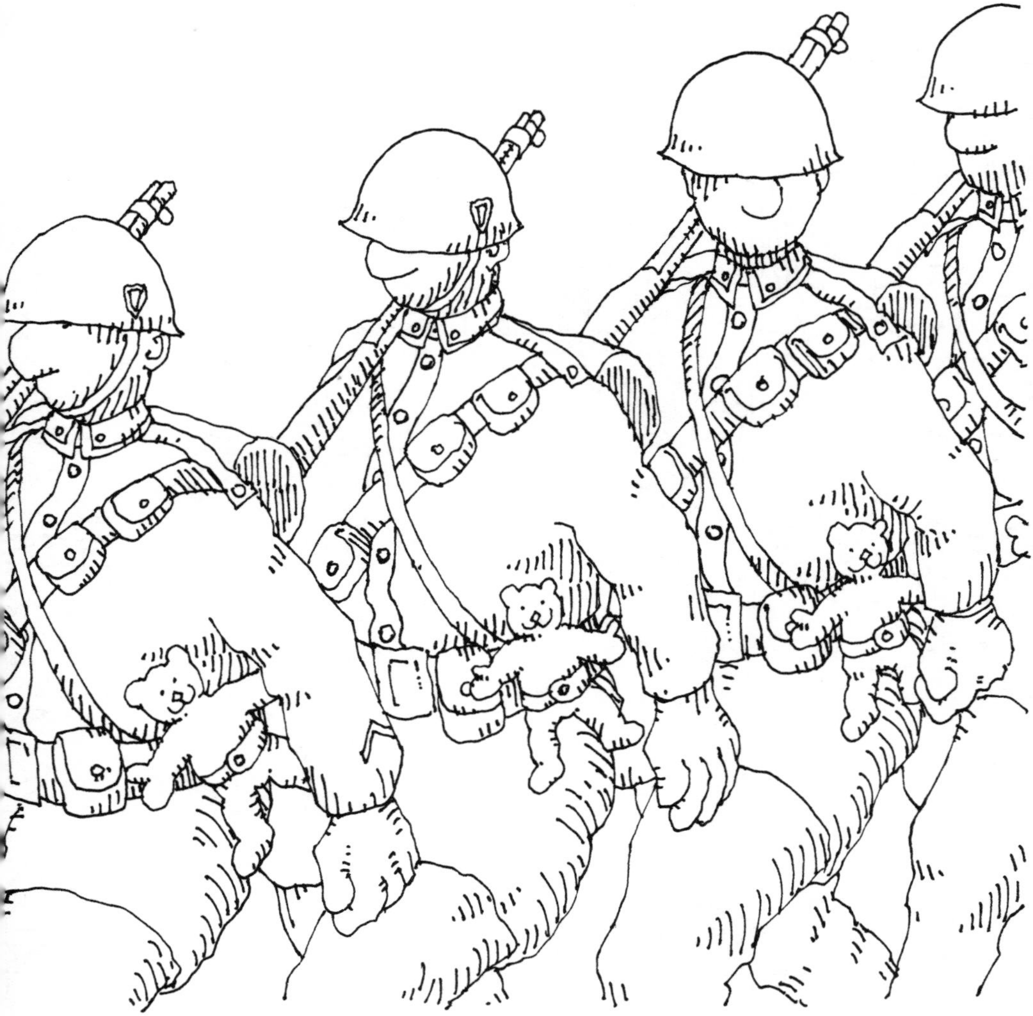

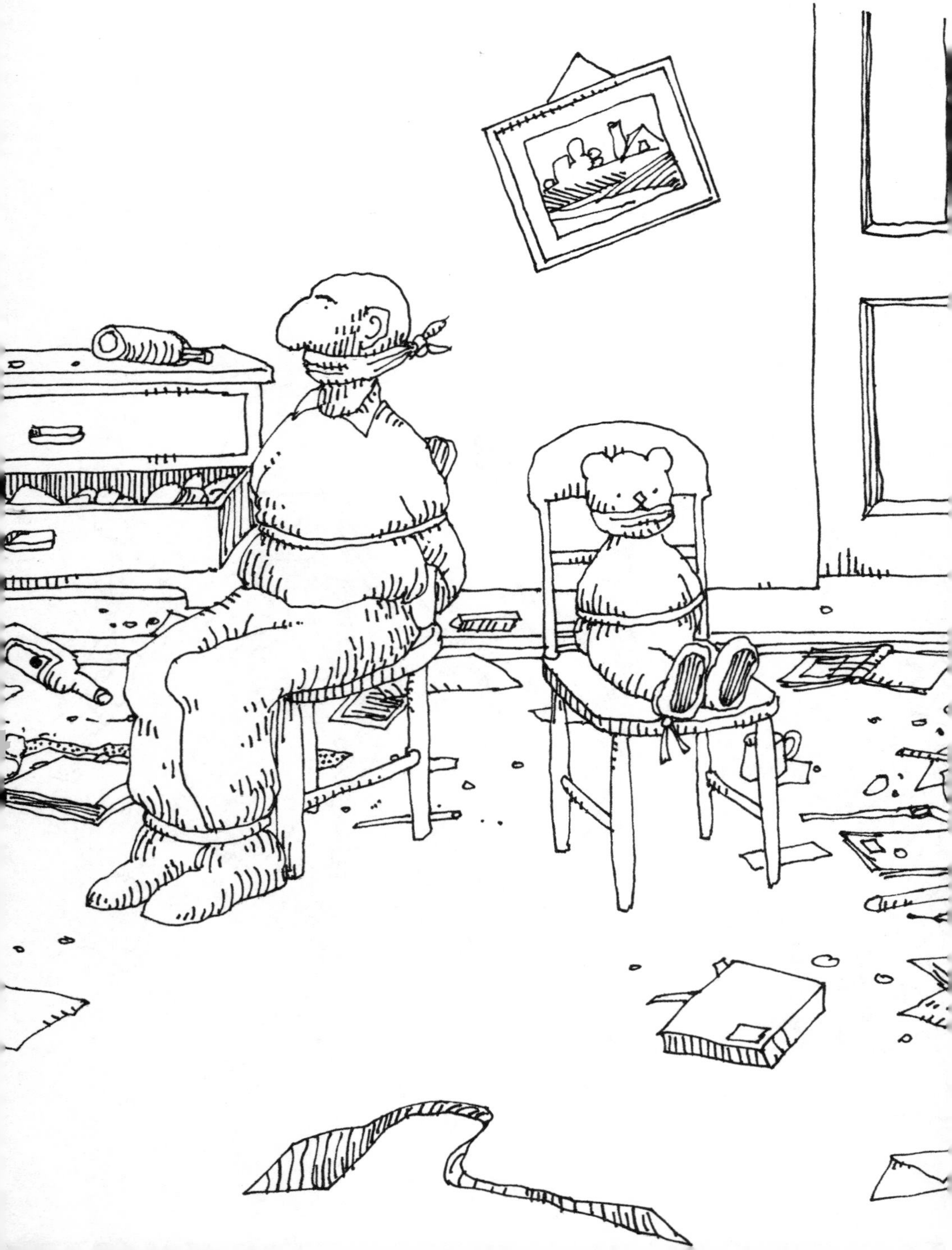

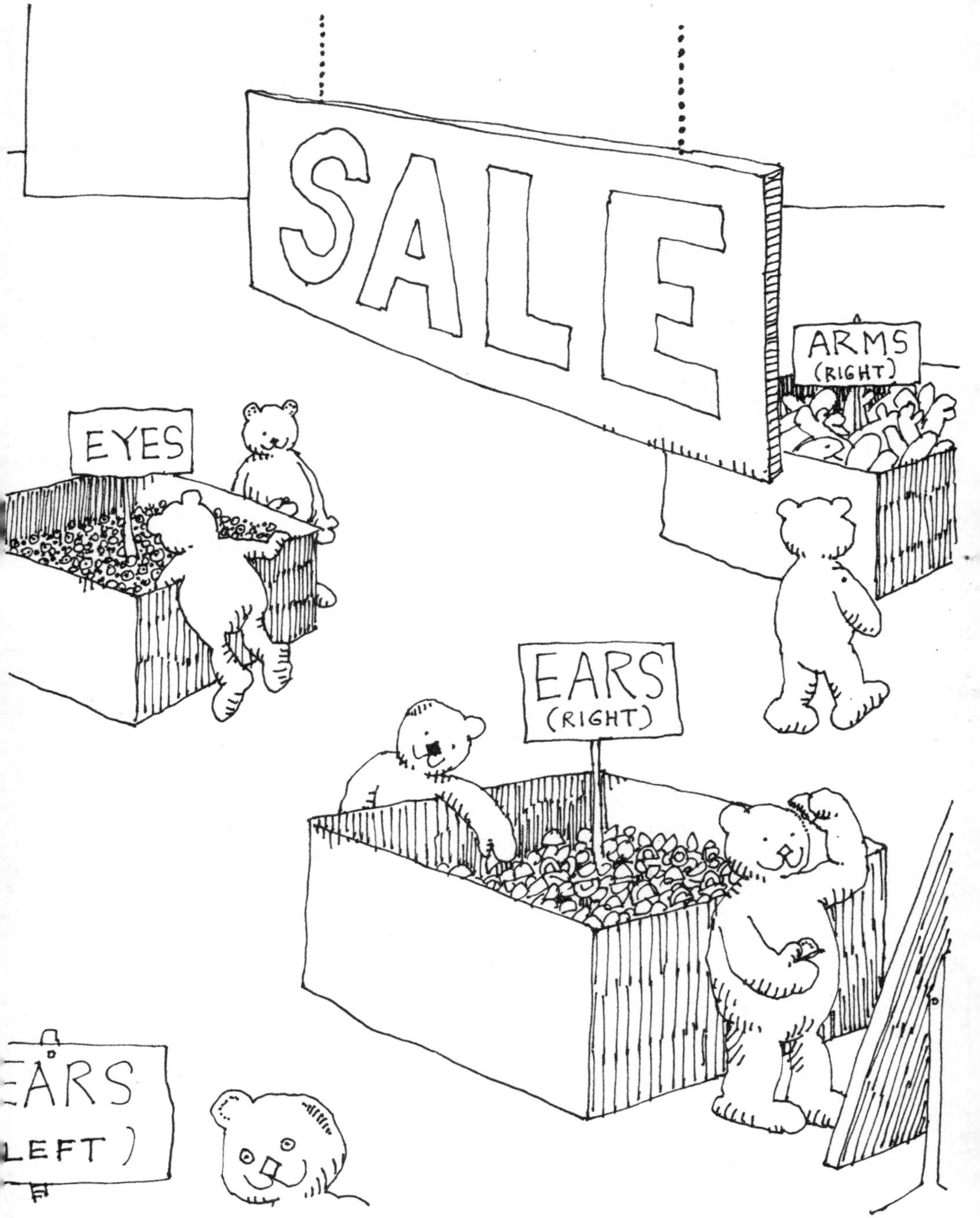
SALE
EYES
ARMS (RIGHT)
EARS (RIGHT)
EARS LEFT)

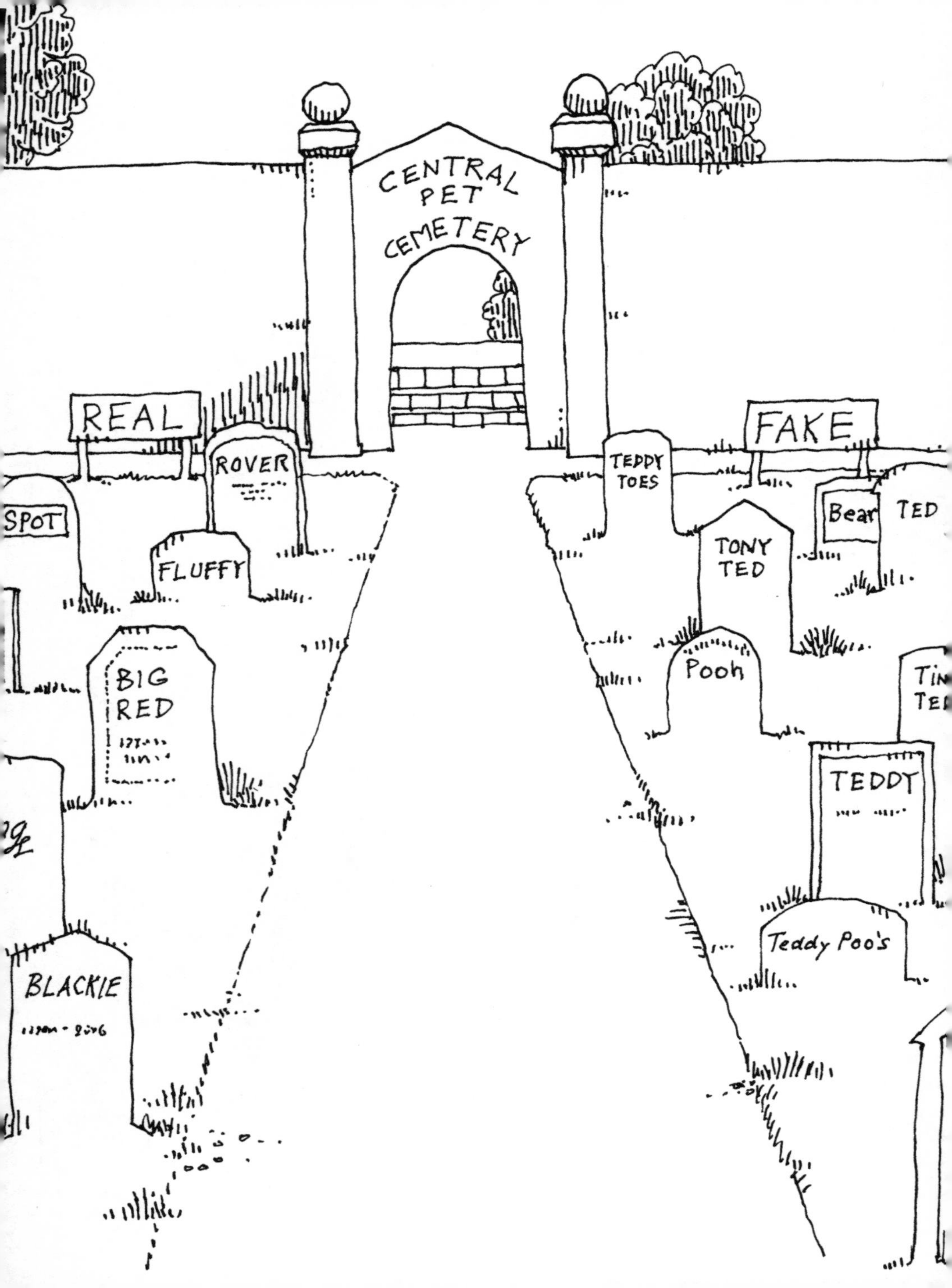
CENTRAL PET CEMETERY
REAL
FAKE
ROVER
SPOT
FLUFFY
BIG RED
BLACKIE
TEDDY TOES
TONY TED
Bear
TED
Pooh
TEDDY
Teddy Poo's

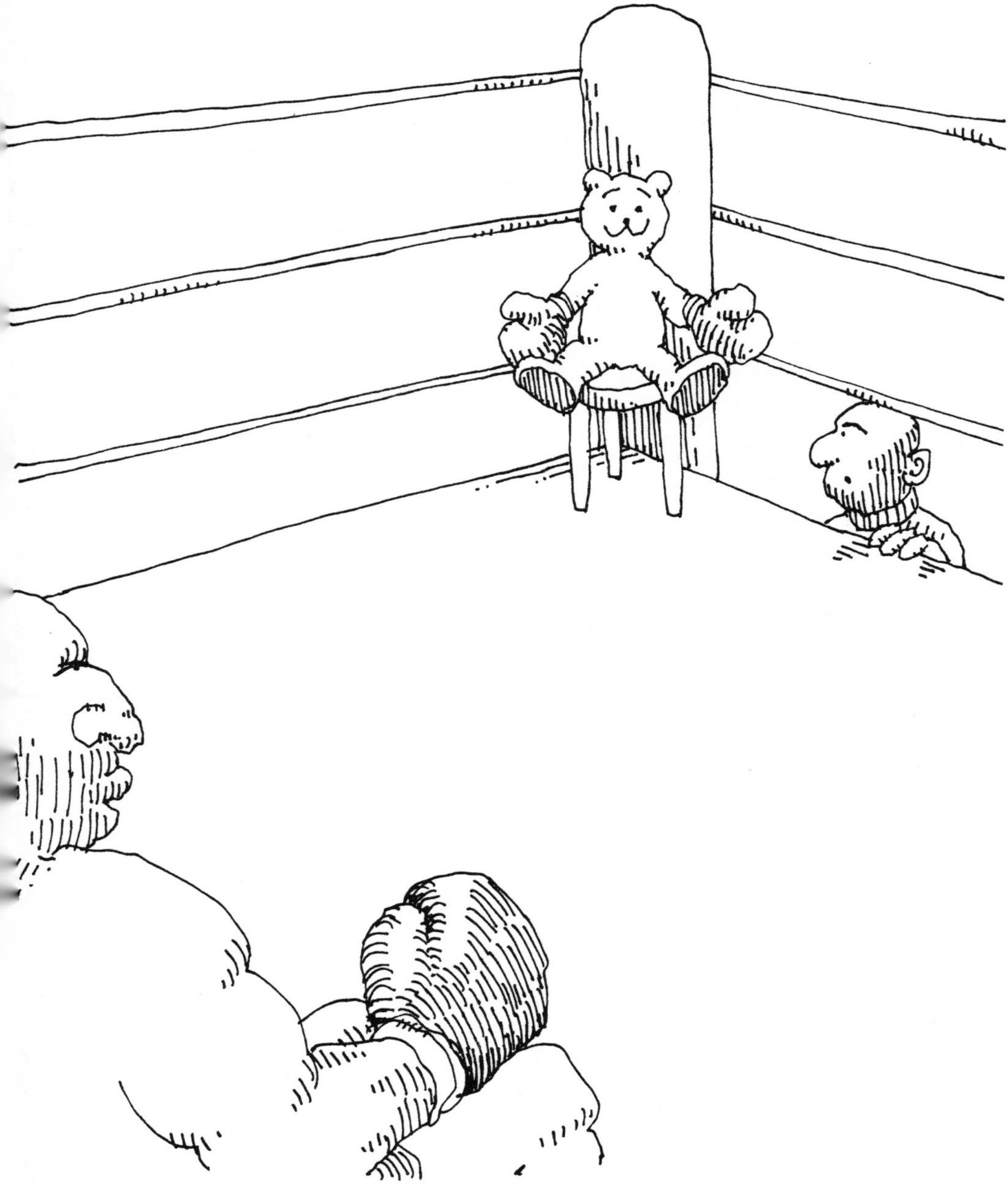

'This is gonna be a tough one, kid!'

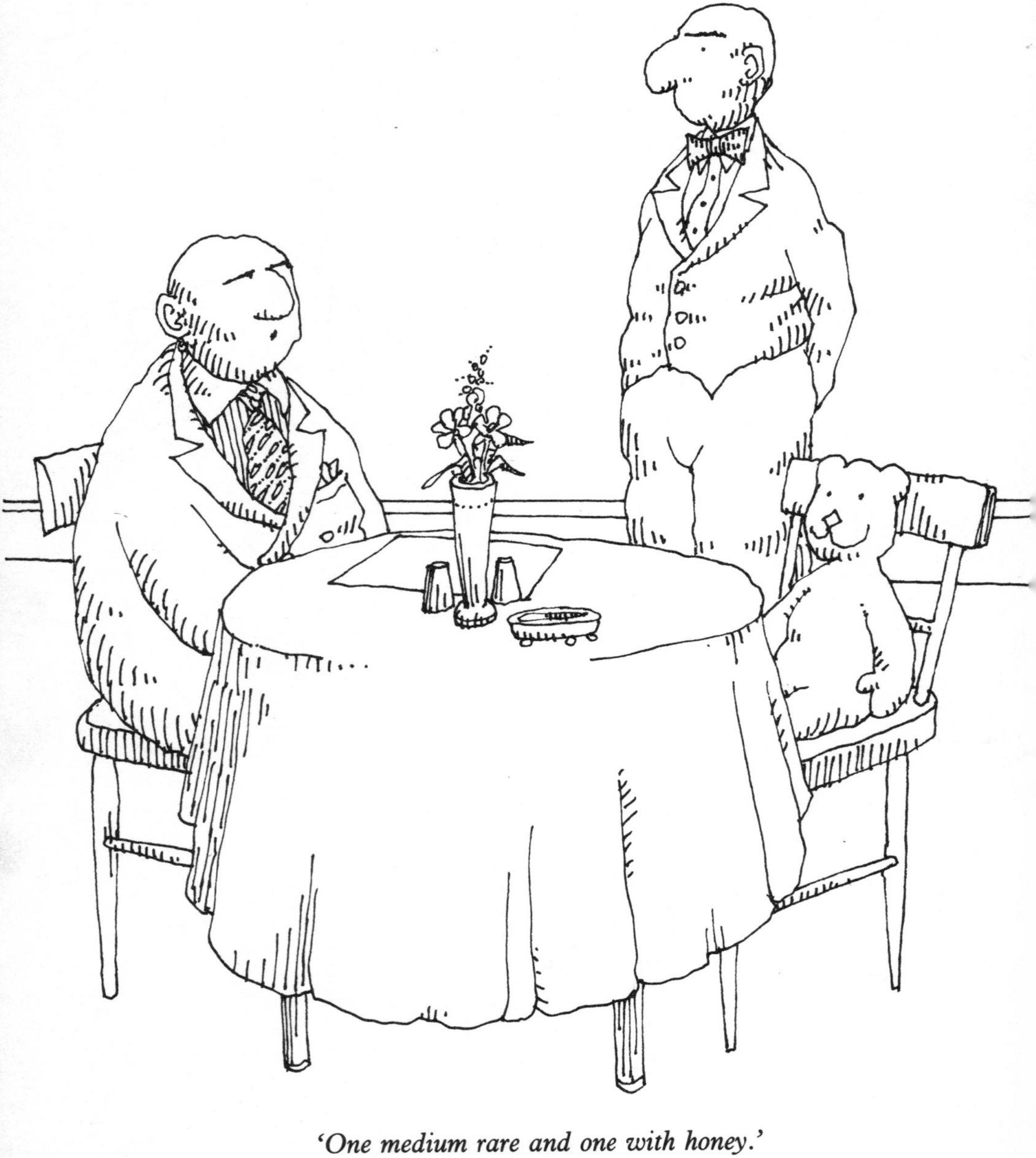

'One medium rare and one with honey.'

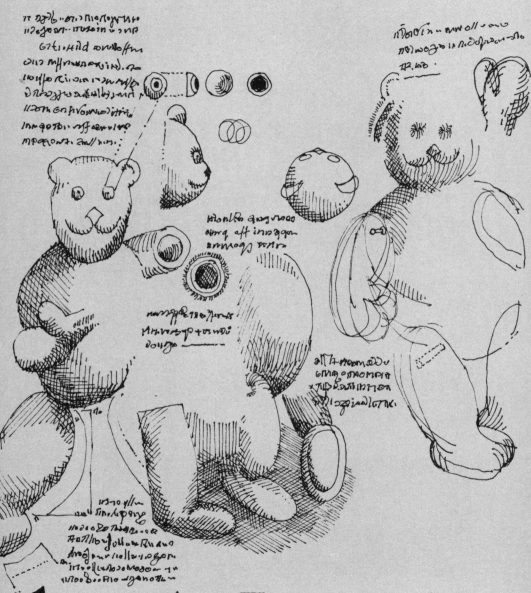

Leonardo's First drawings

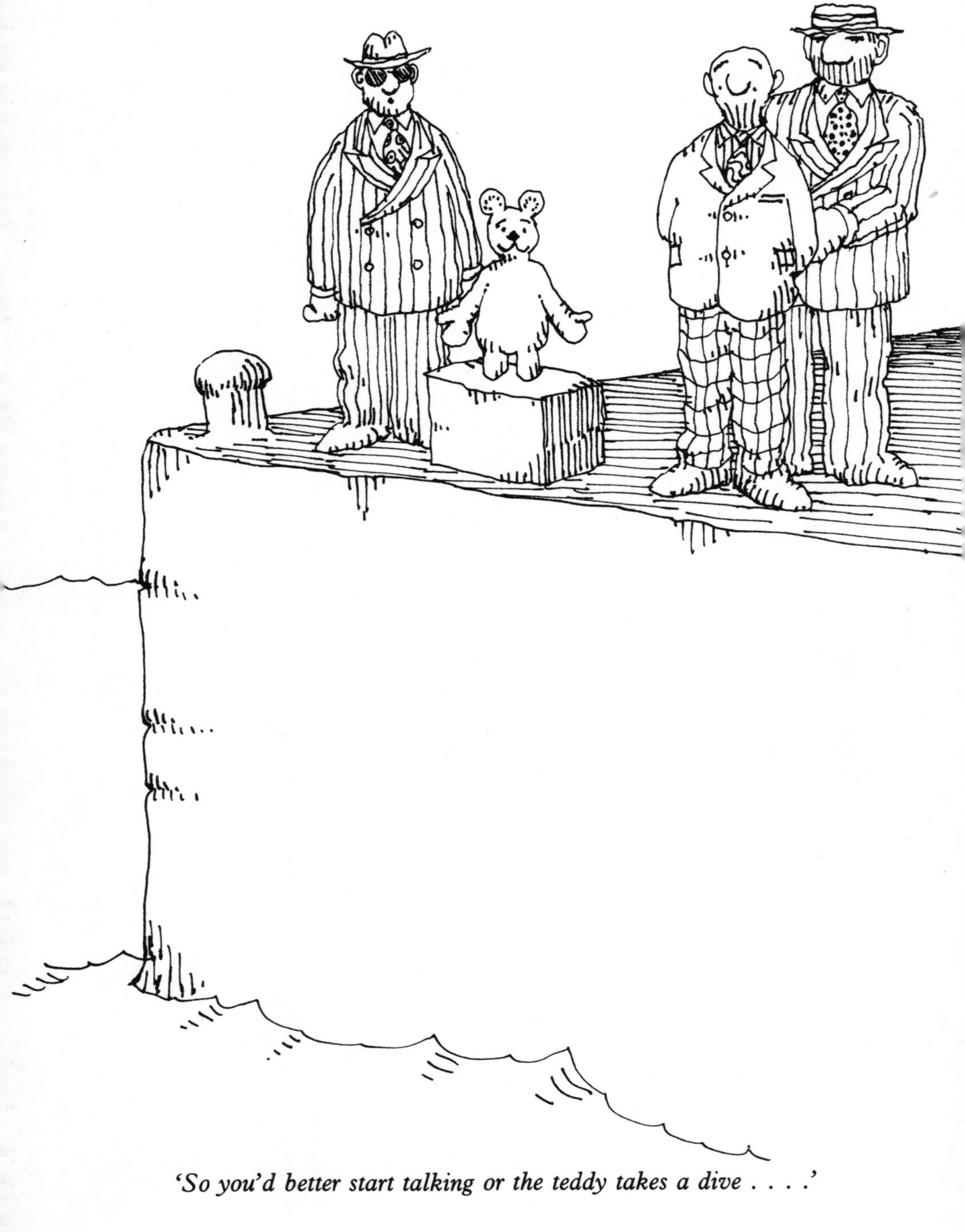

'So you'd better start talking or the teddy takes a dive . . . .'

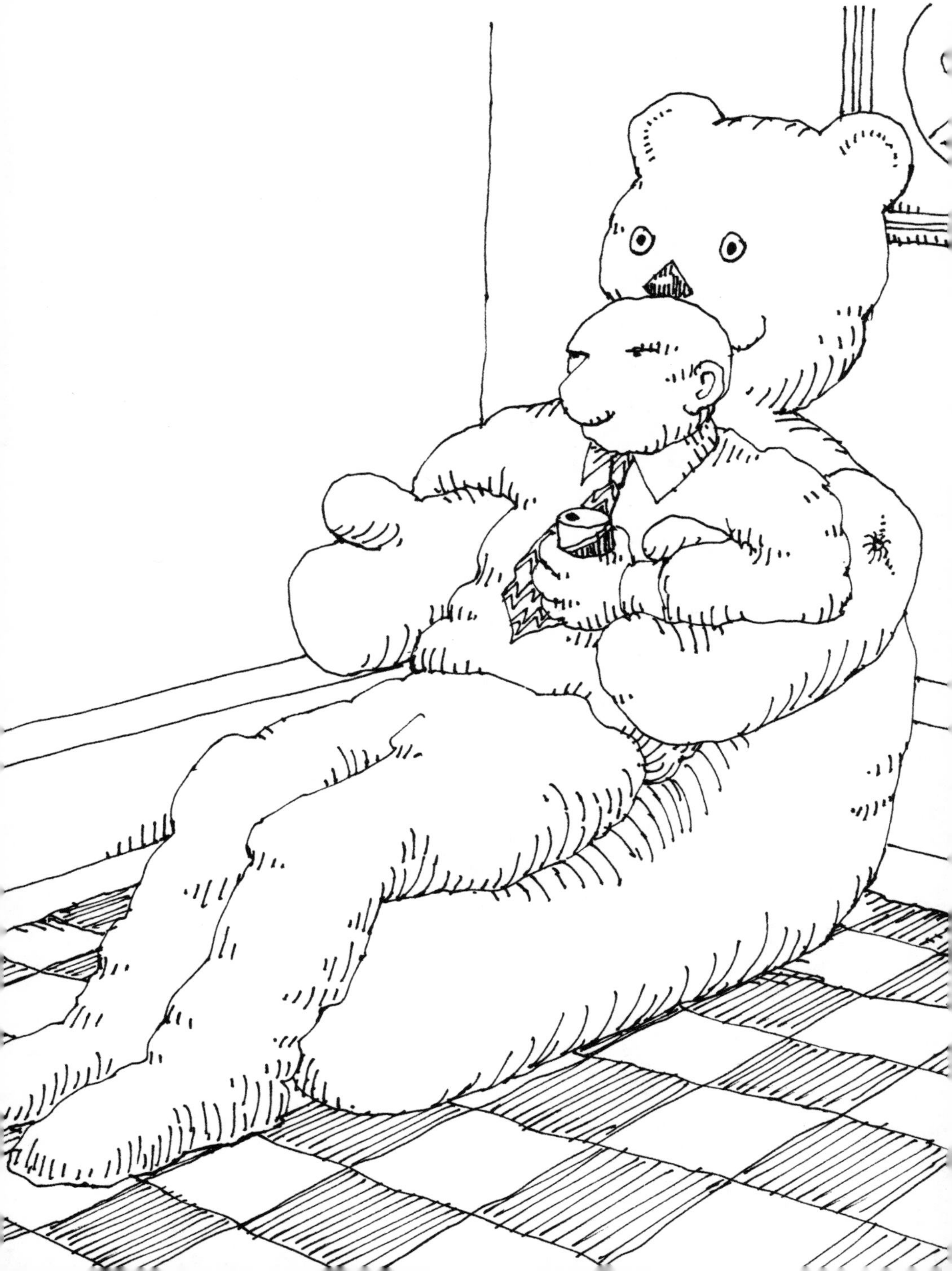

THE NICE NAZIS

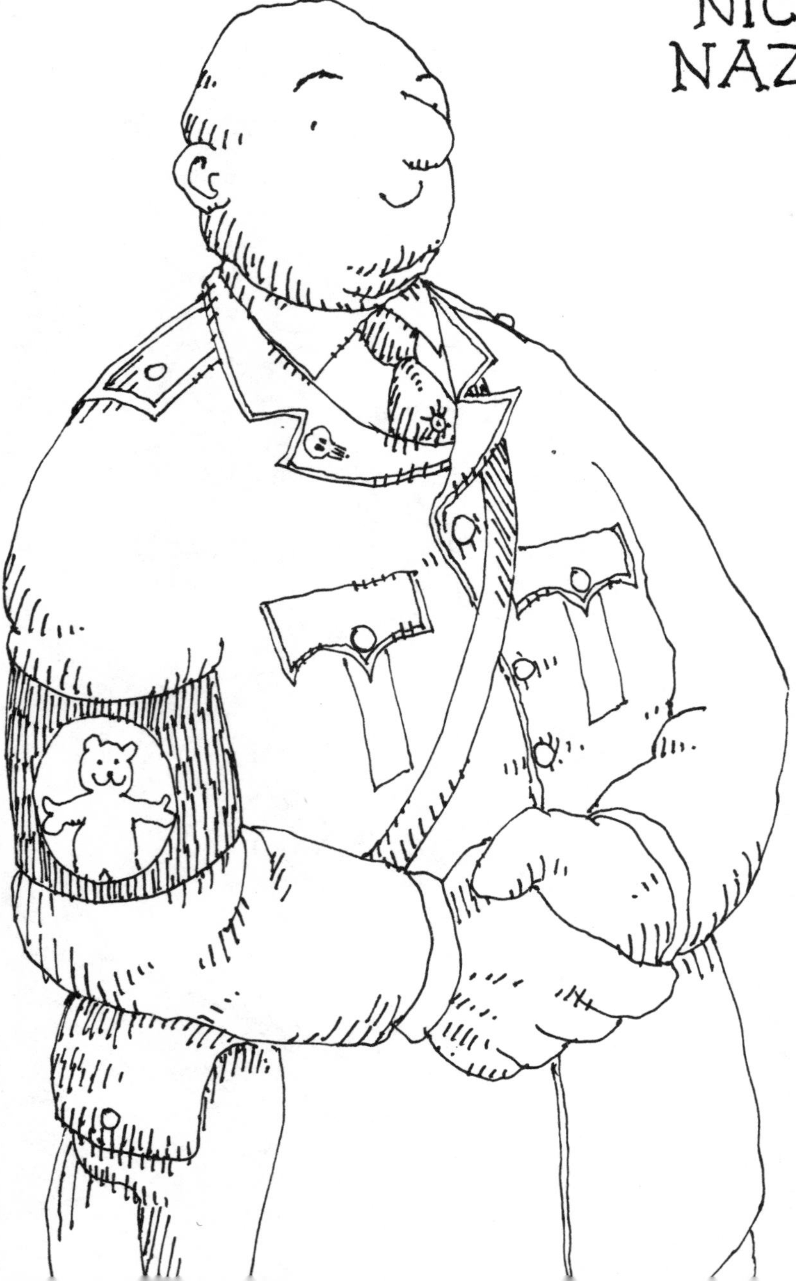

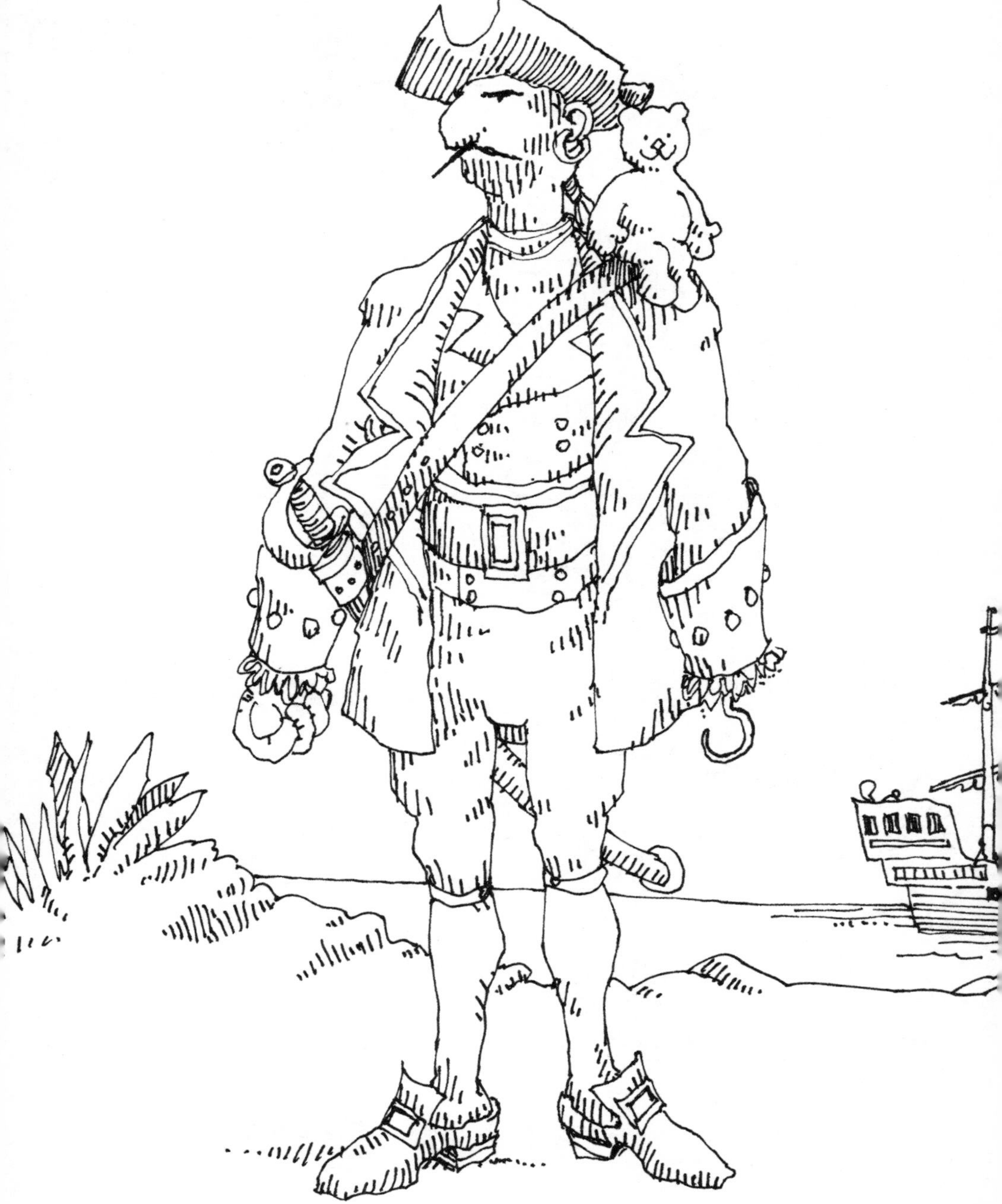

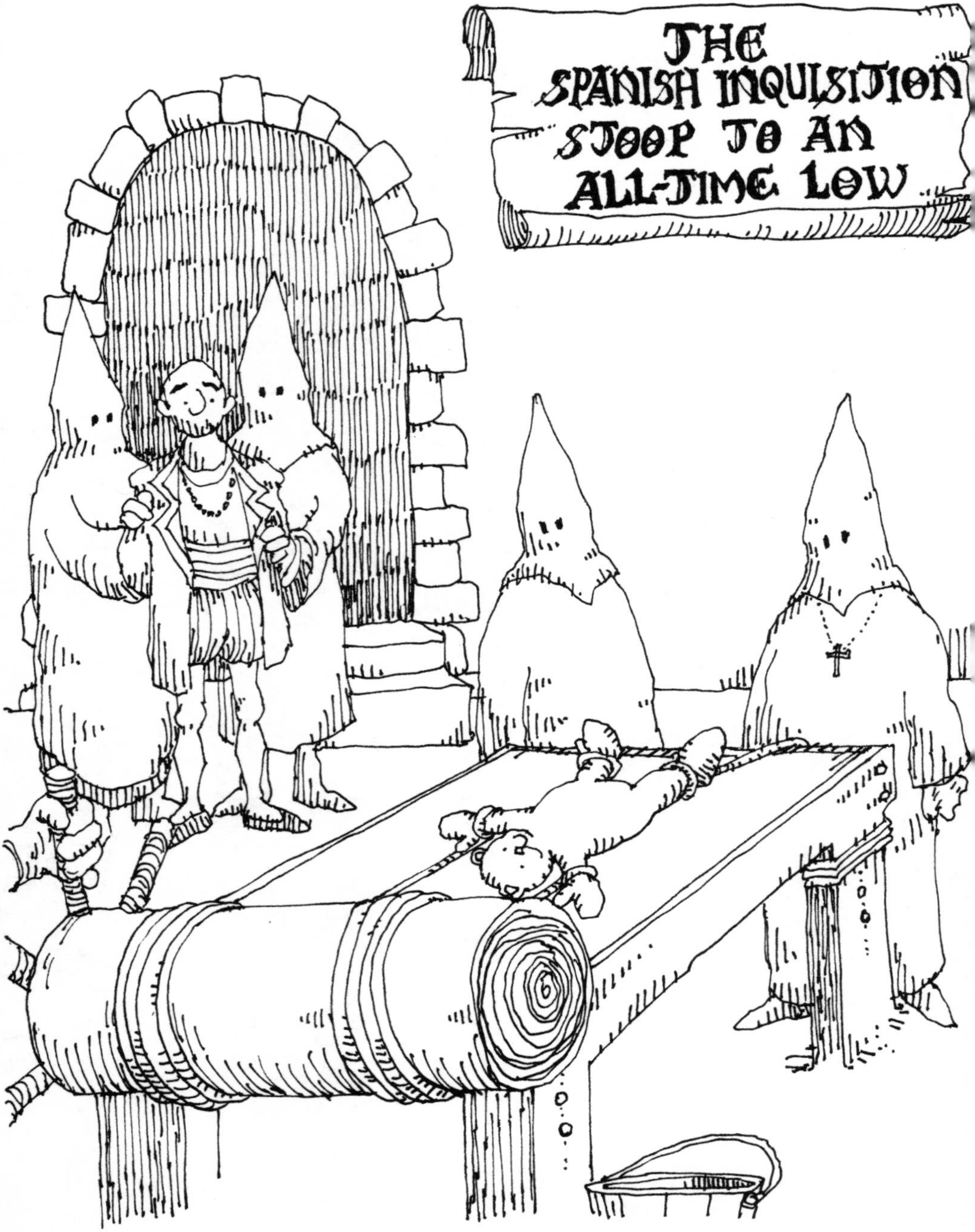

THE SPANISH INQUISITION STOOP TO AN ALL-TIME LOW

IN CASE OF
ANXIETY
BREAK GLASS

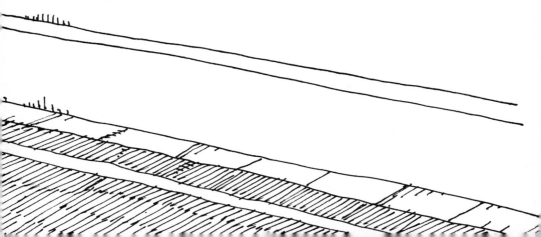

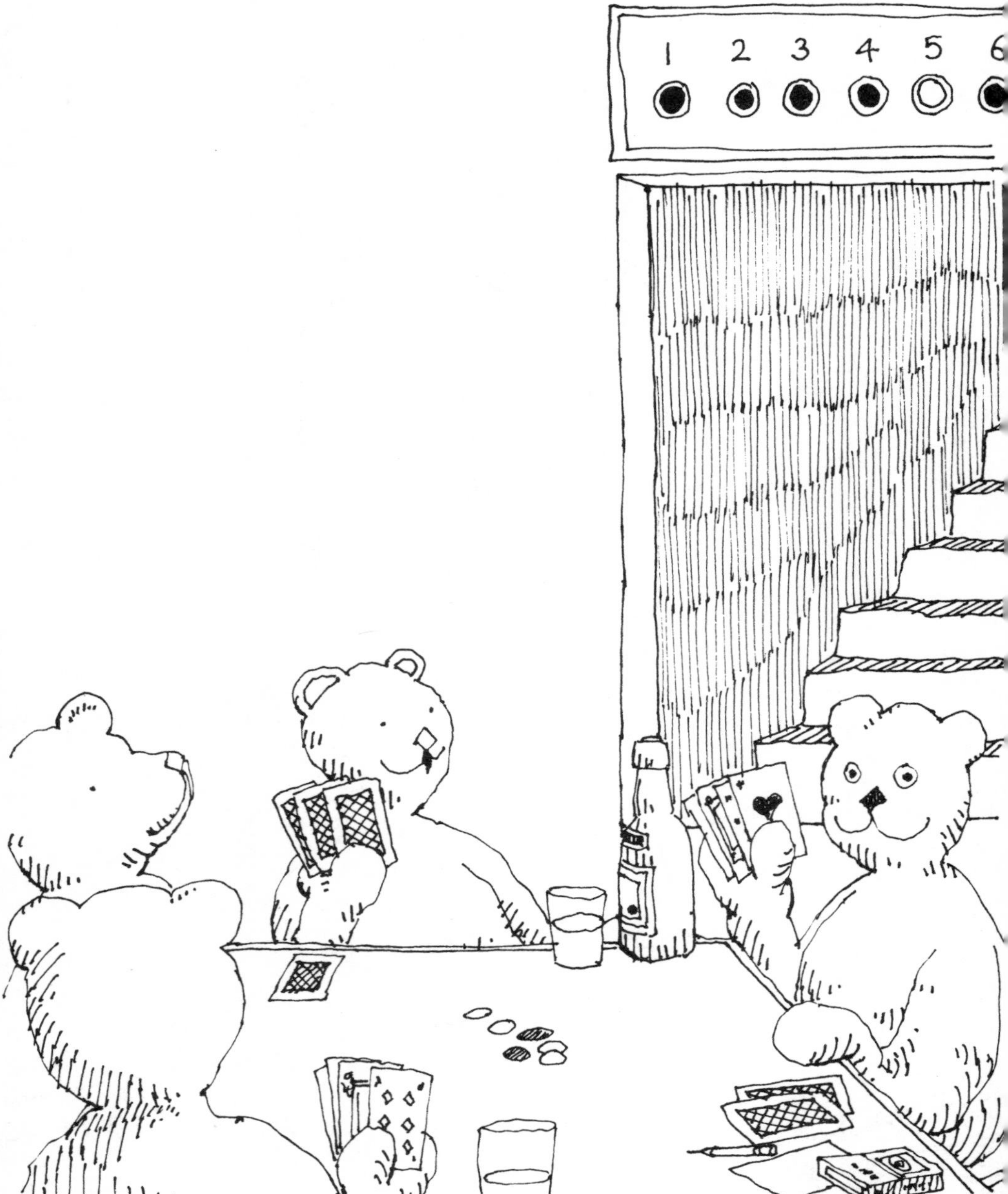
1
2
3
4
5
6

'Kid awake in number five.'

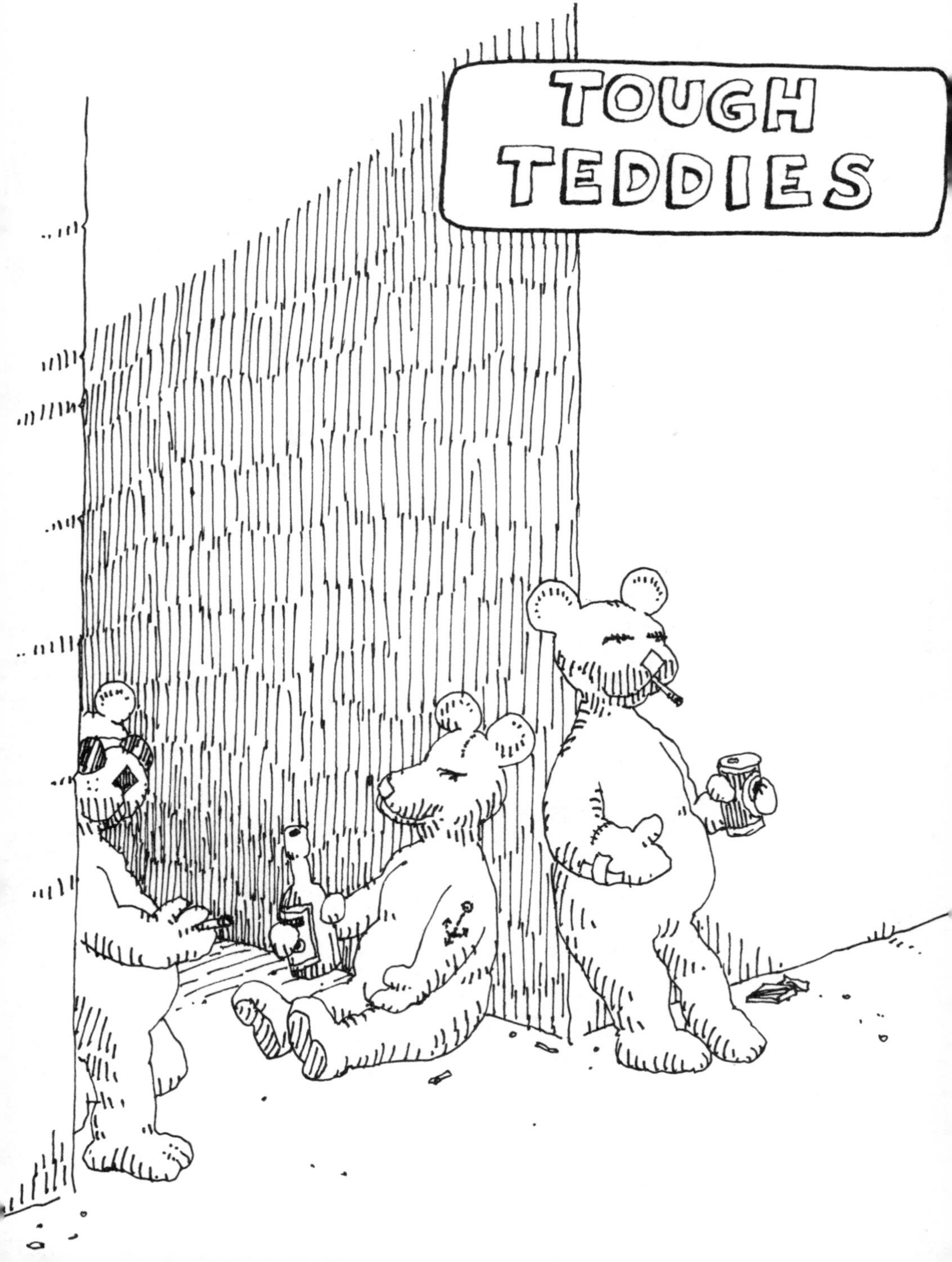
TOUGH TEDDIES

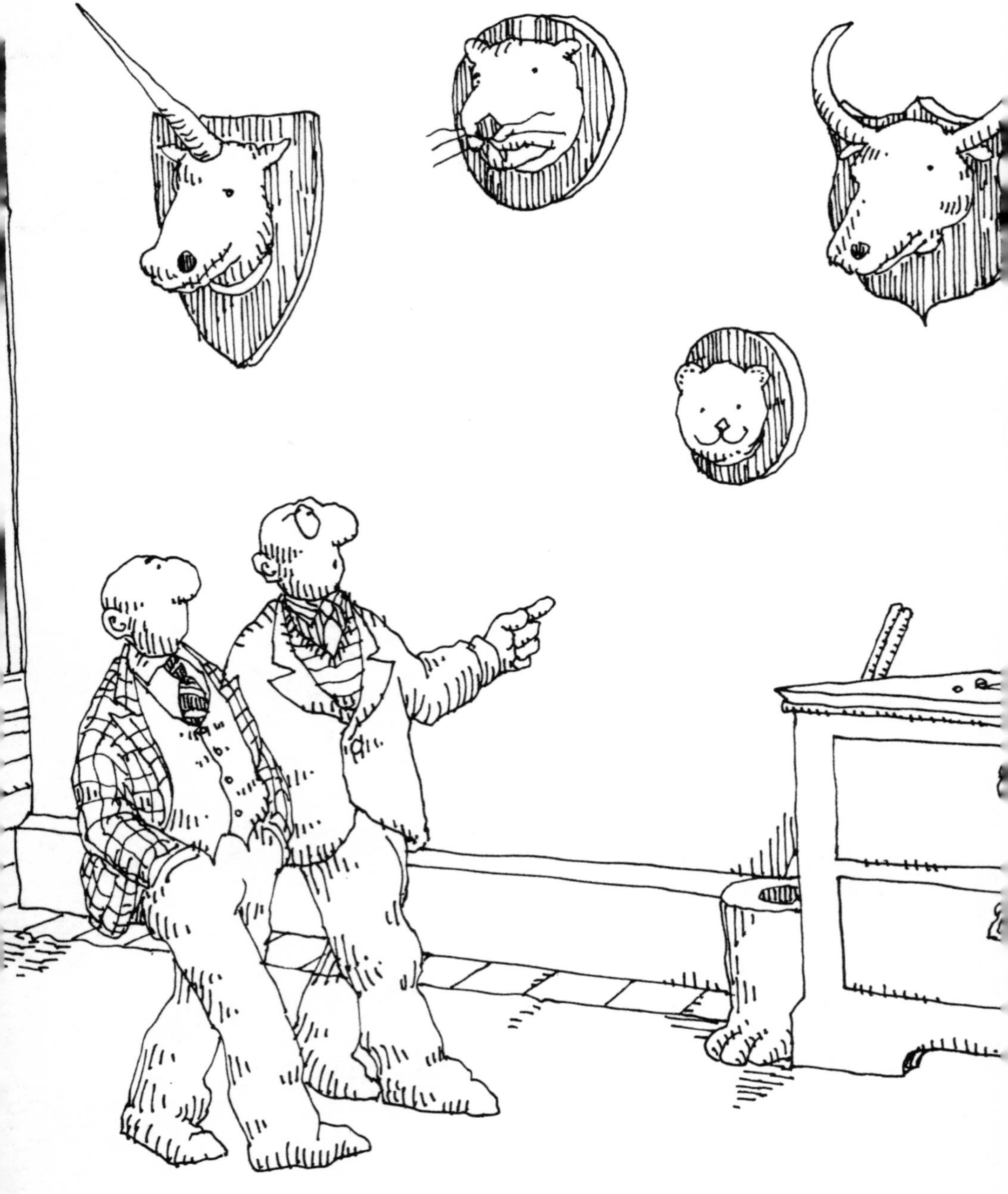

'And this one I got in the nursery in '34.'

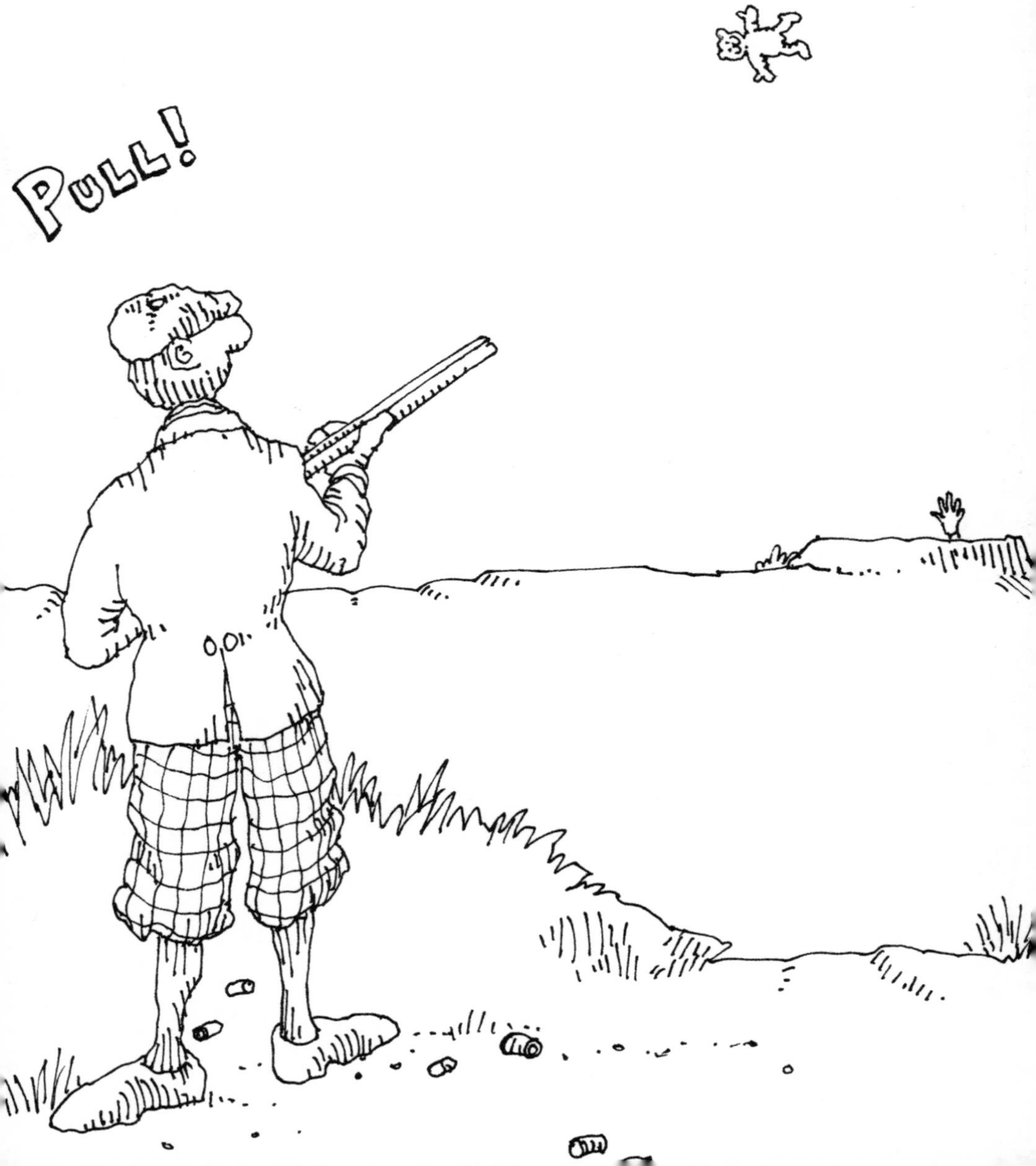
PULL!

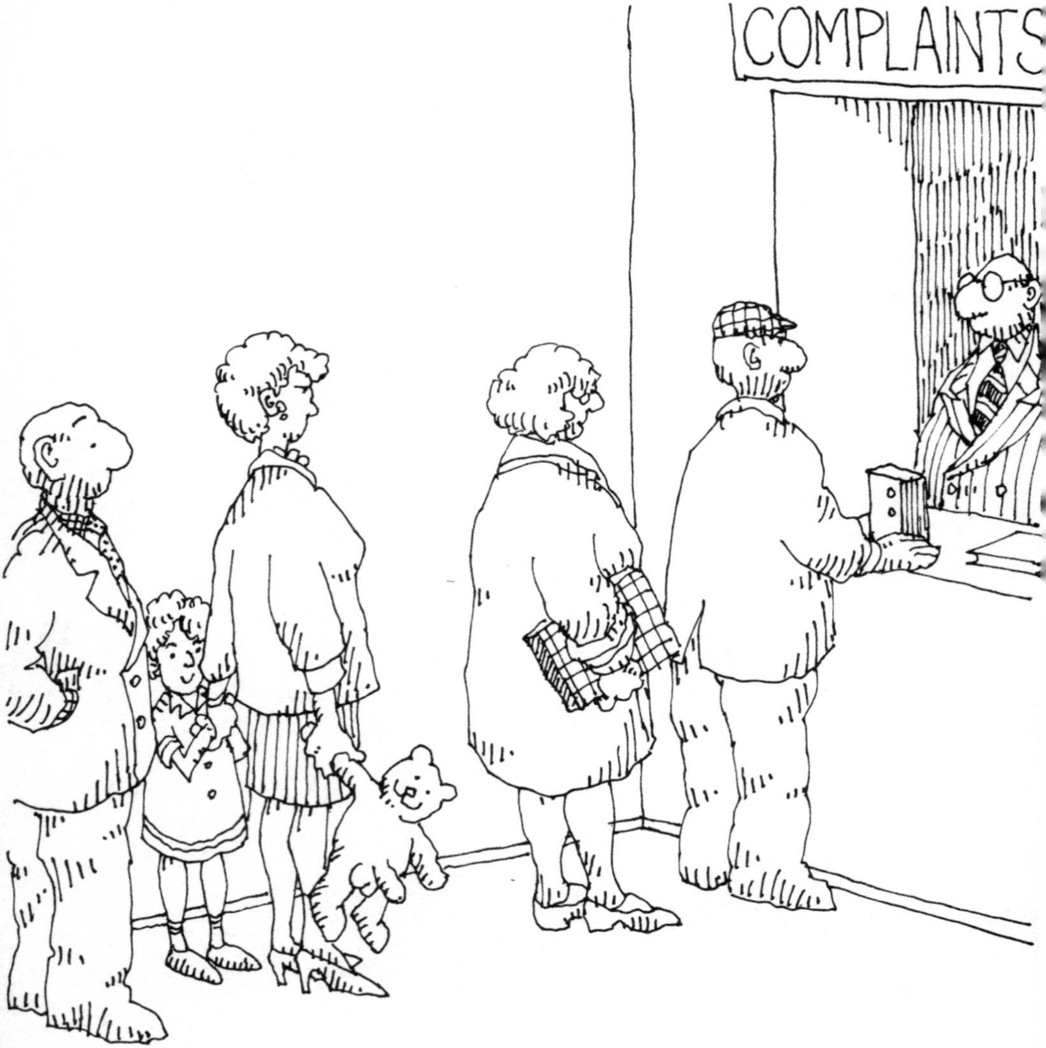
COMPLAINTS

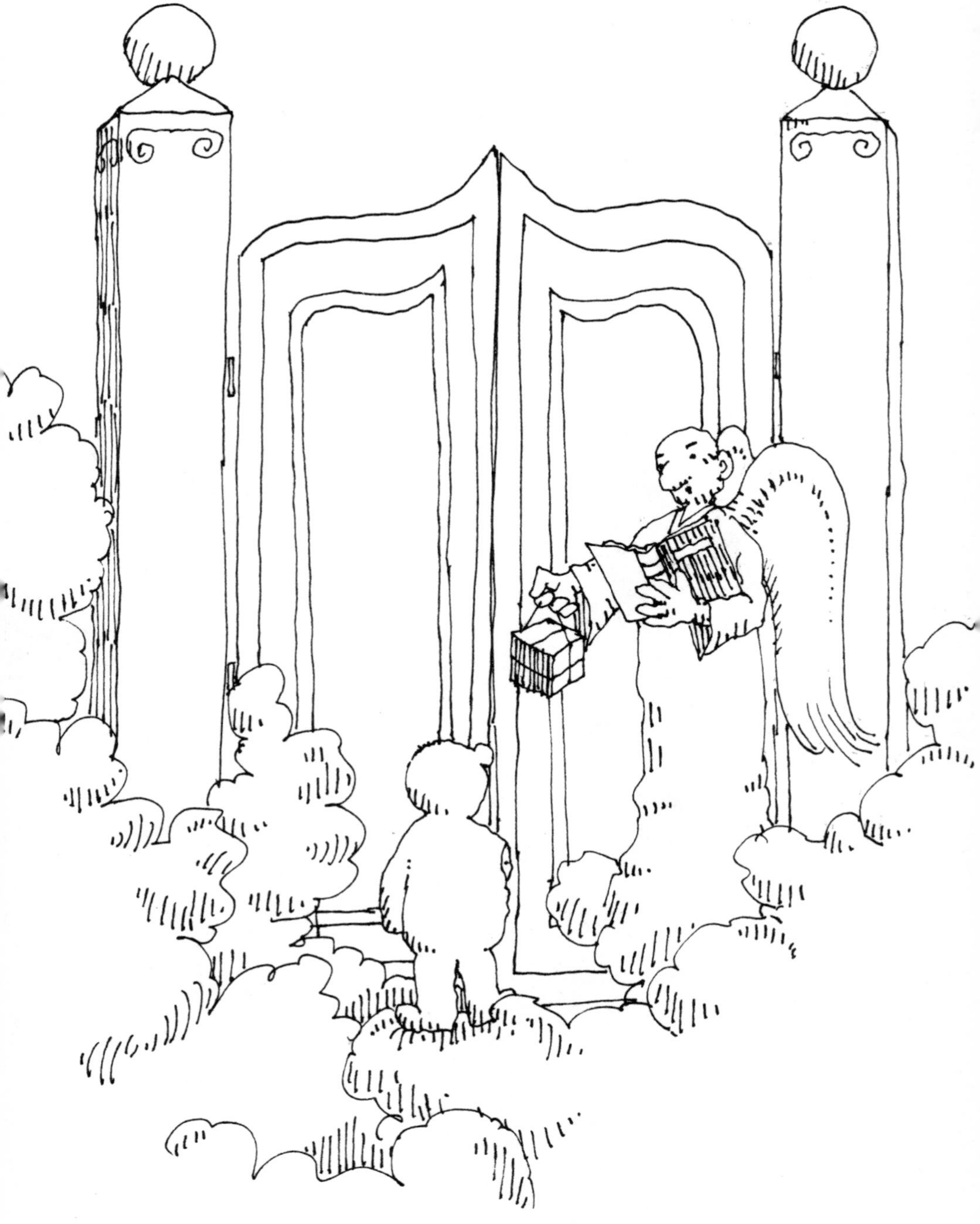

'Welcome and here is your ear and arm back.'

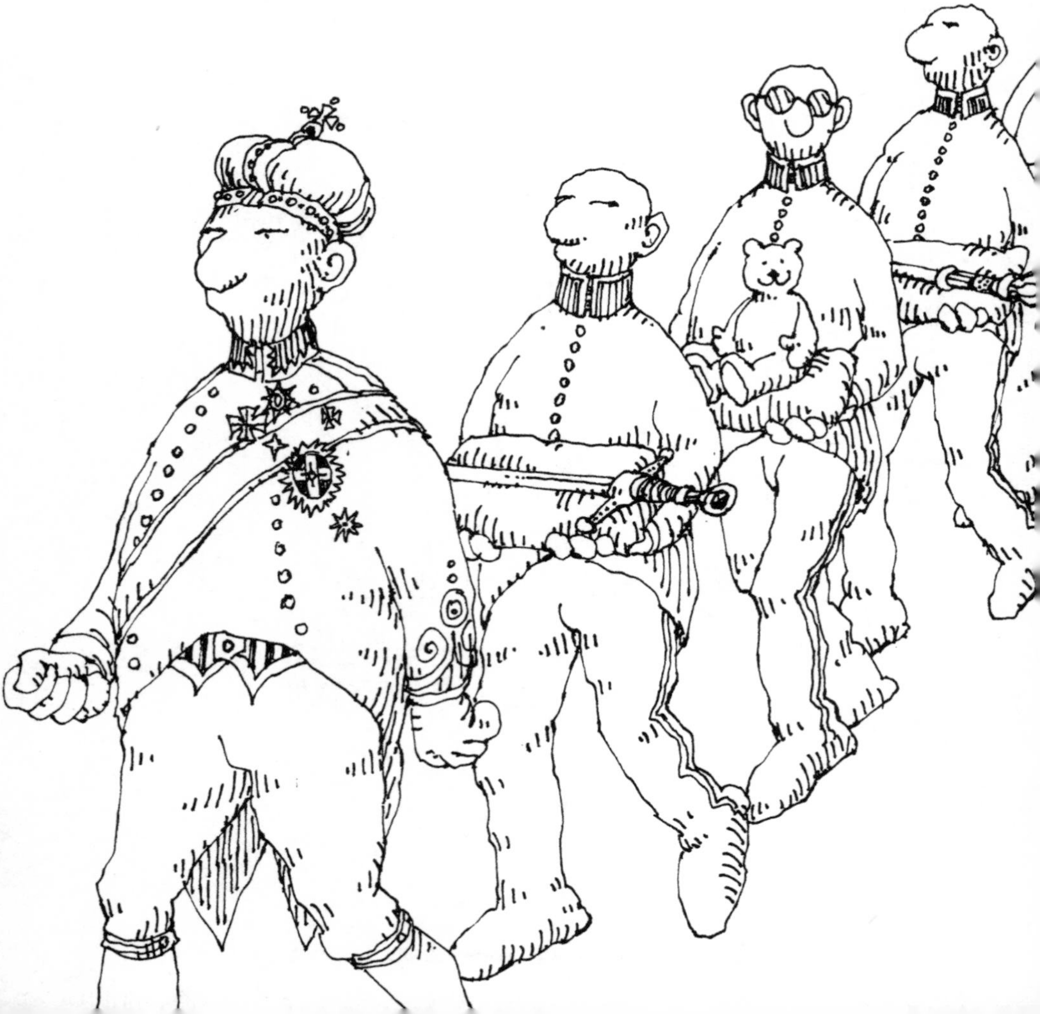

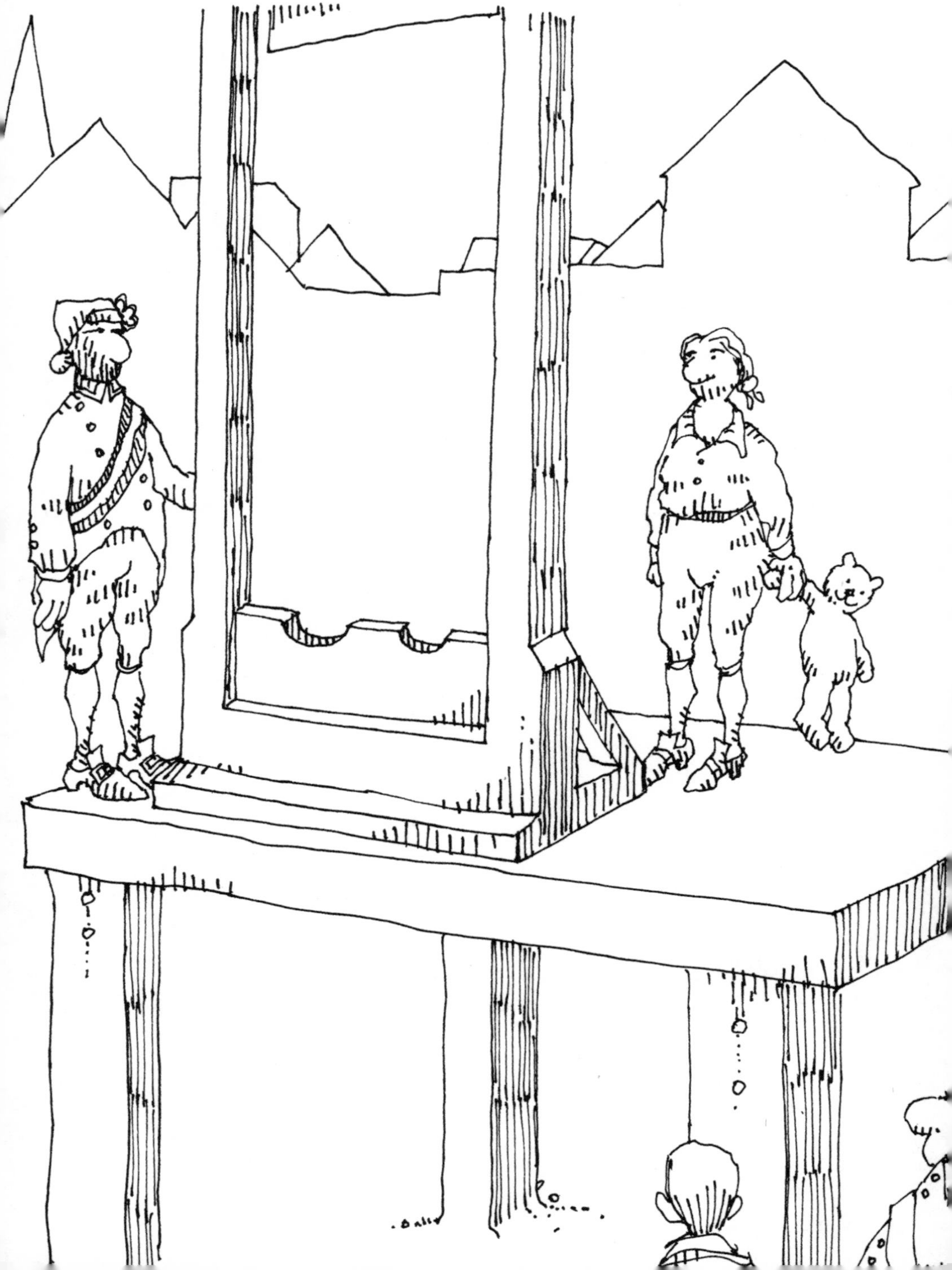

Foiled Again!

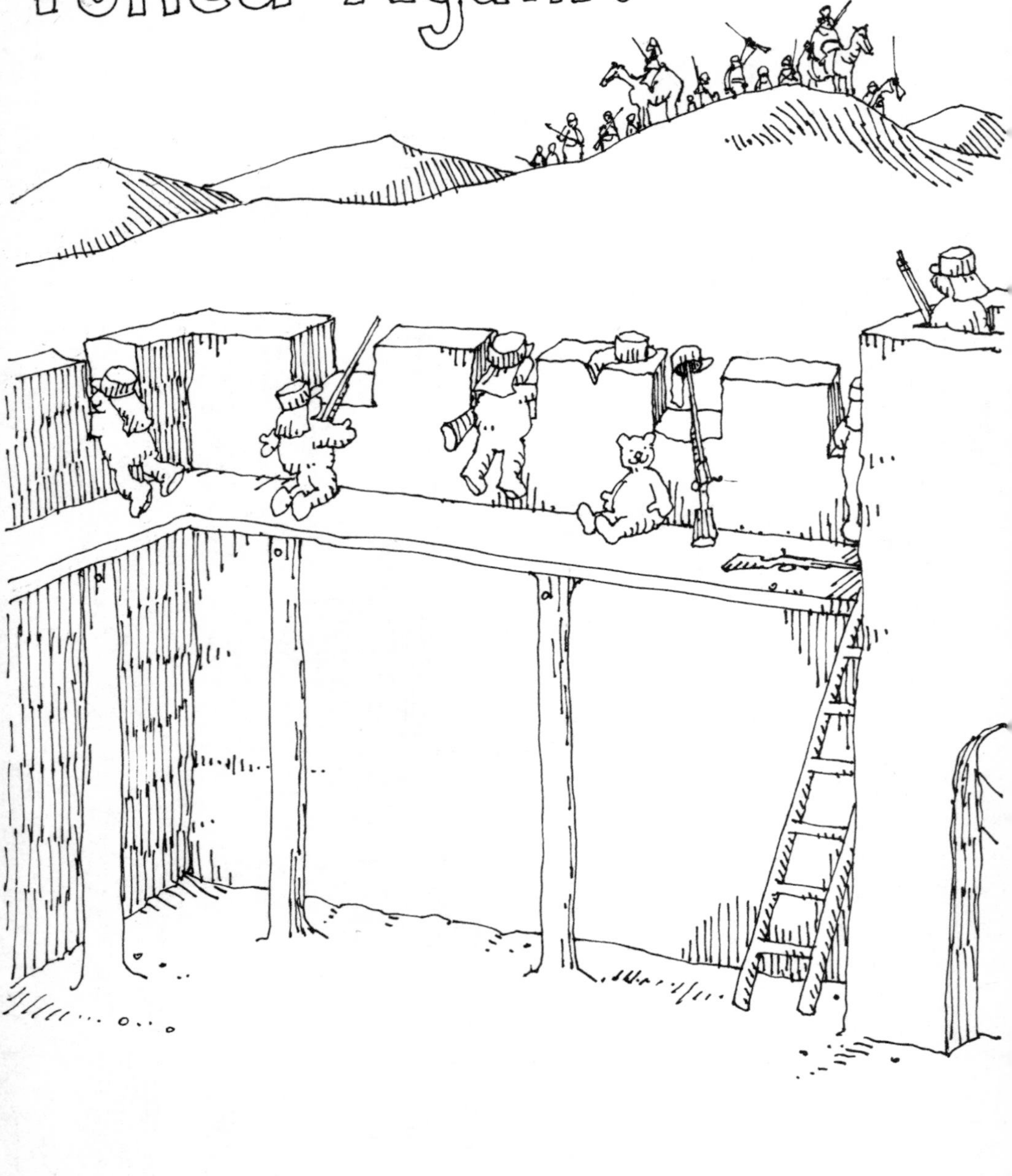

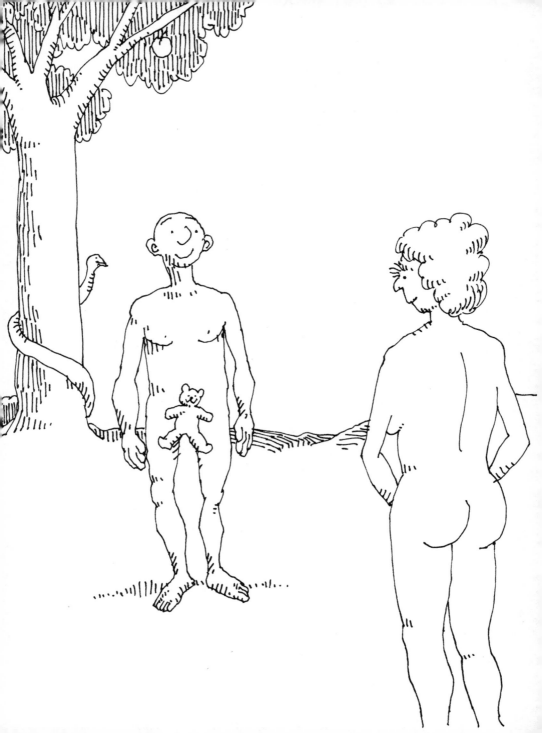

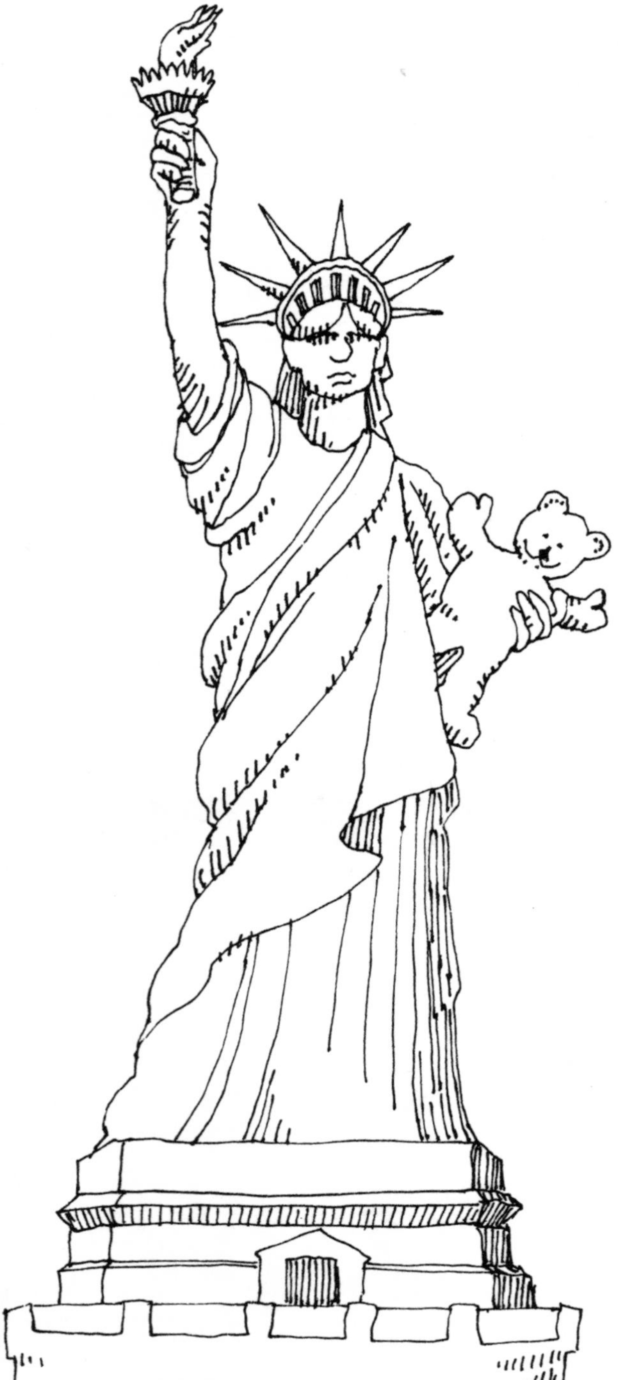

ROMULUS & REMUS
(AND THEIR BROTHER DEREK)

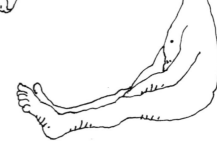

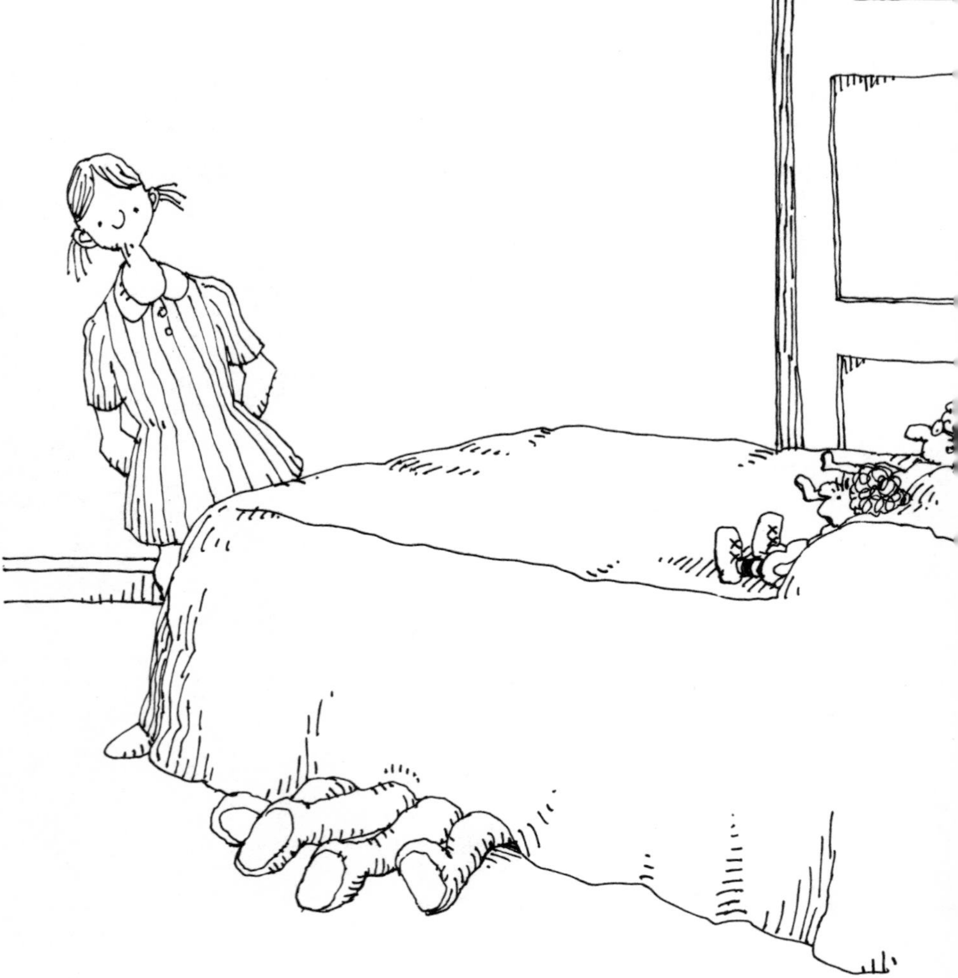

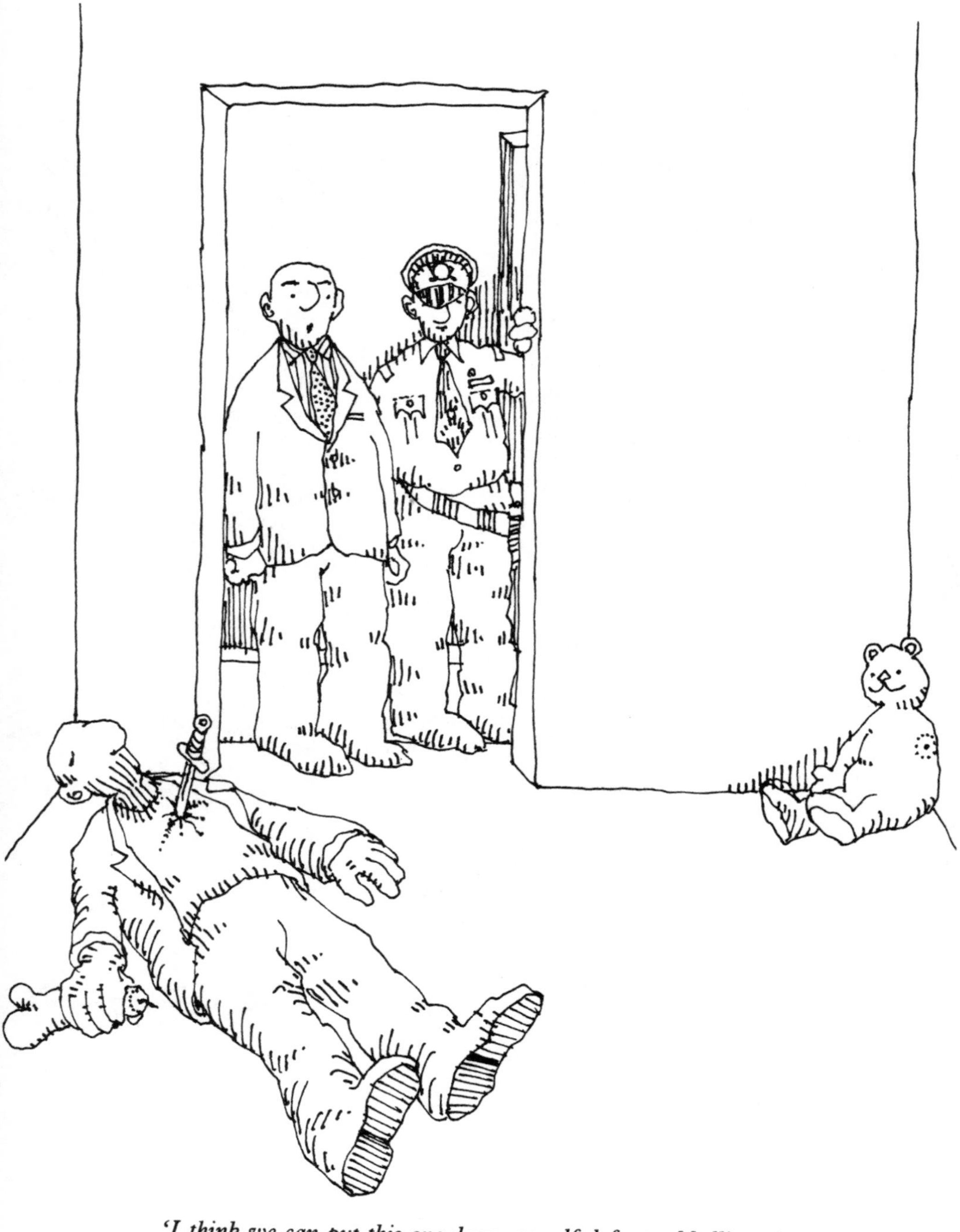

'I think we can put this one down as self-defence, Mulligan.'

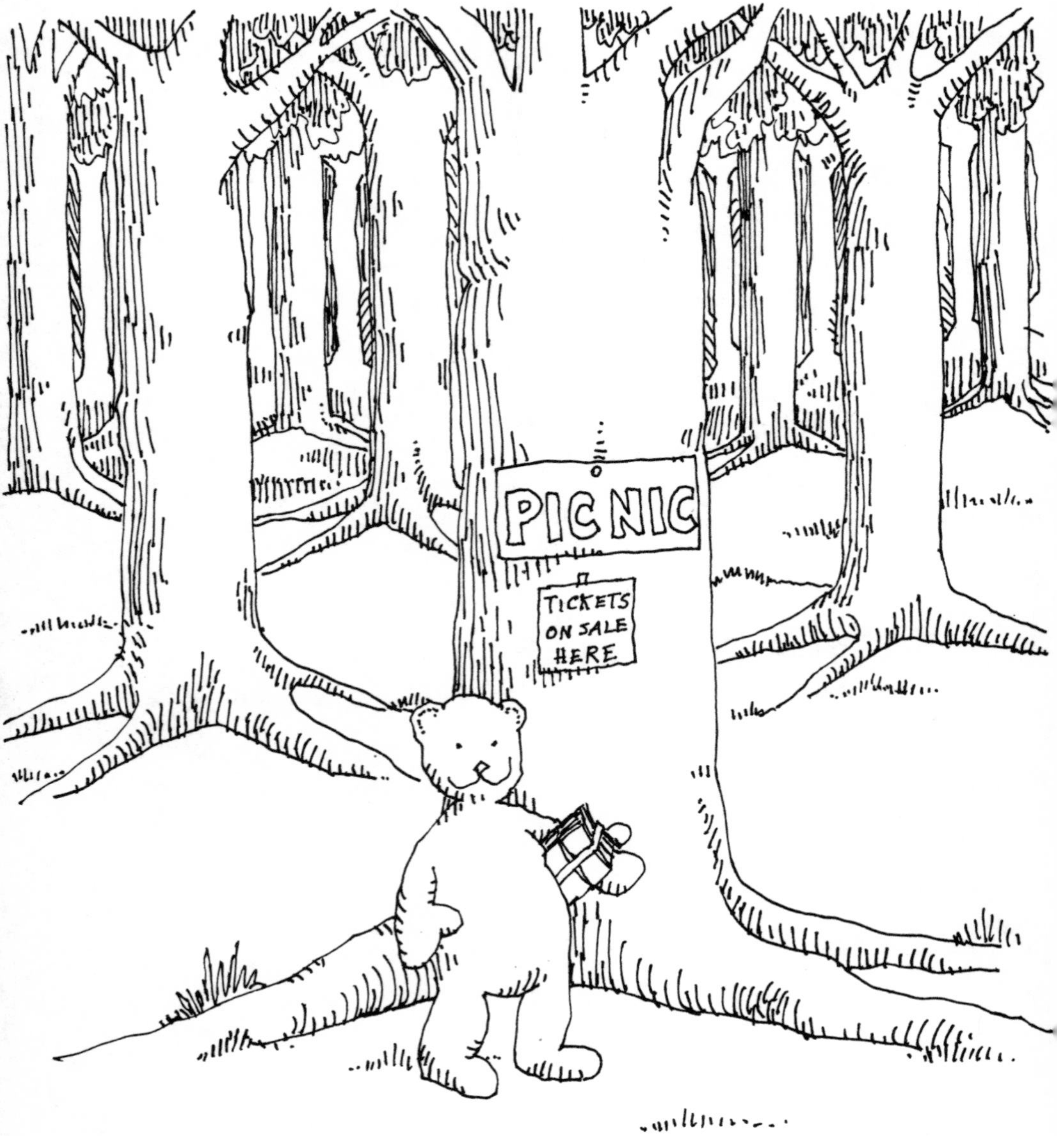
PICNIC
TICKETS ON SALE HERE

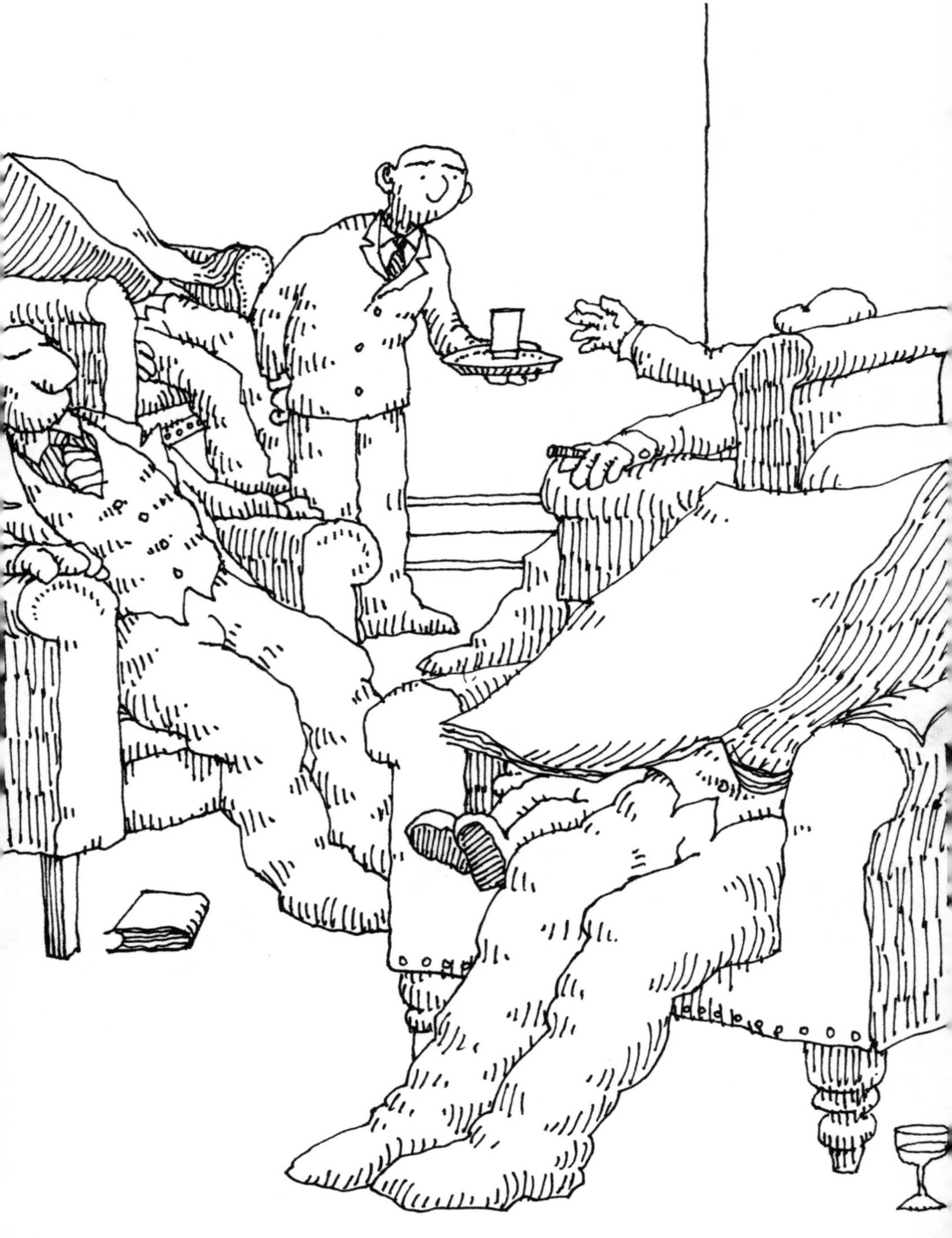

Picasso's teddy

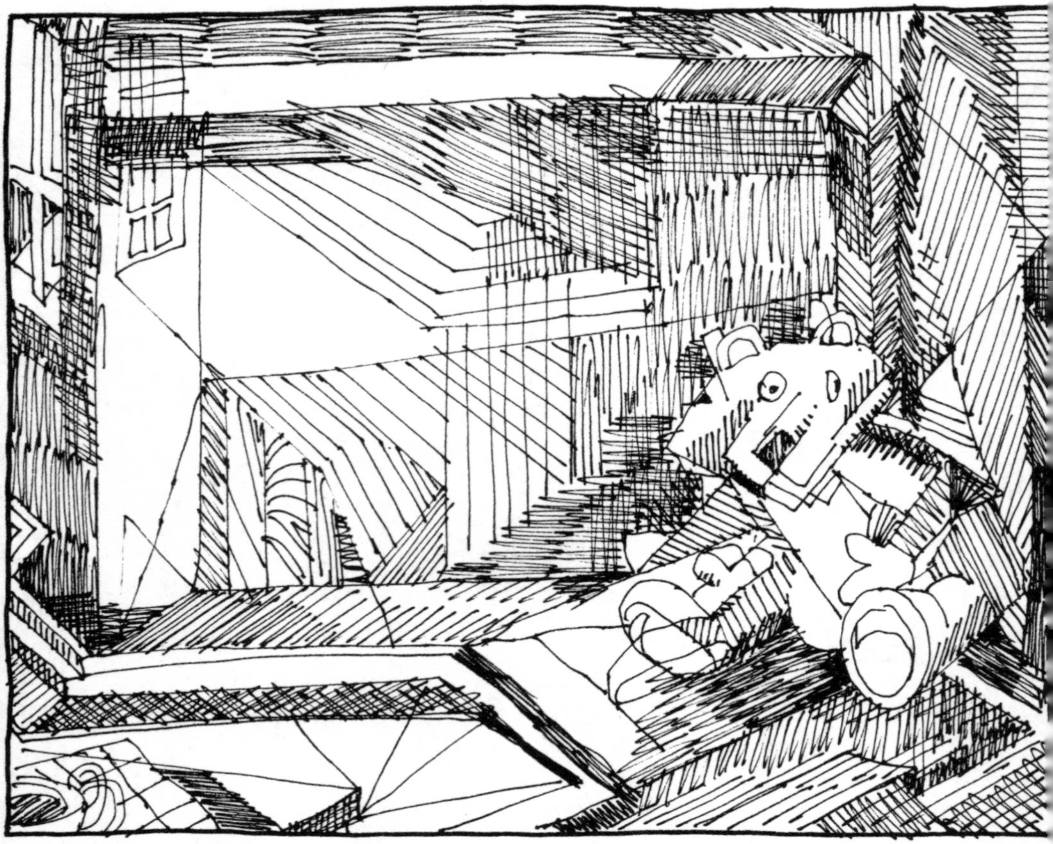

1910

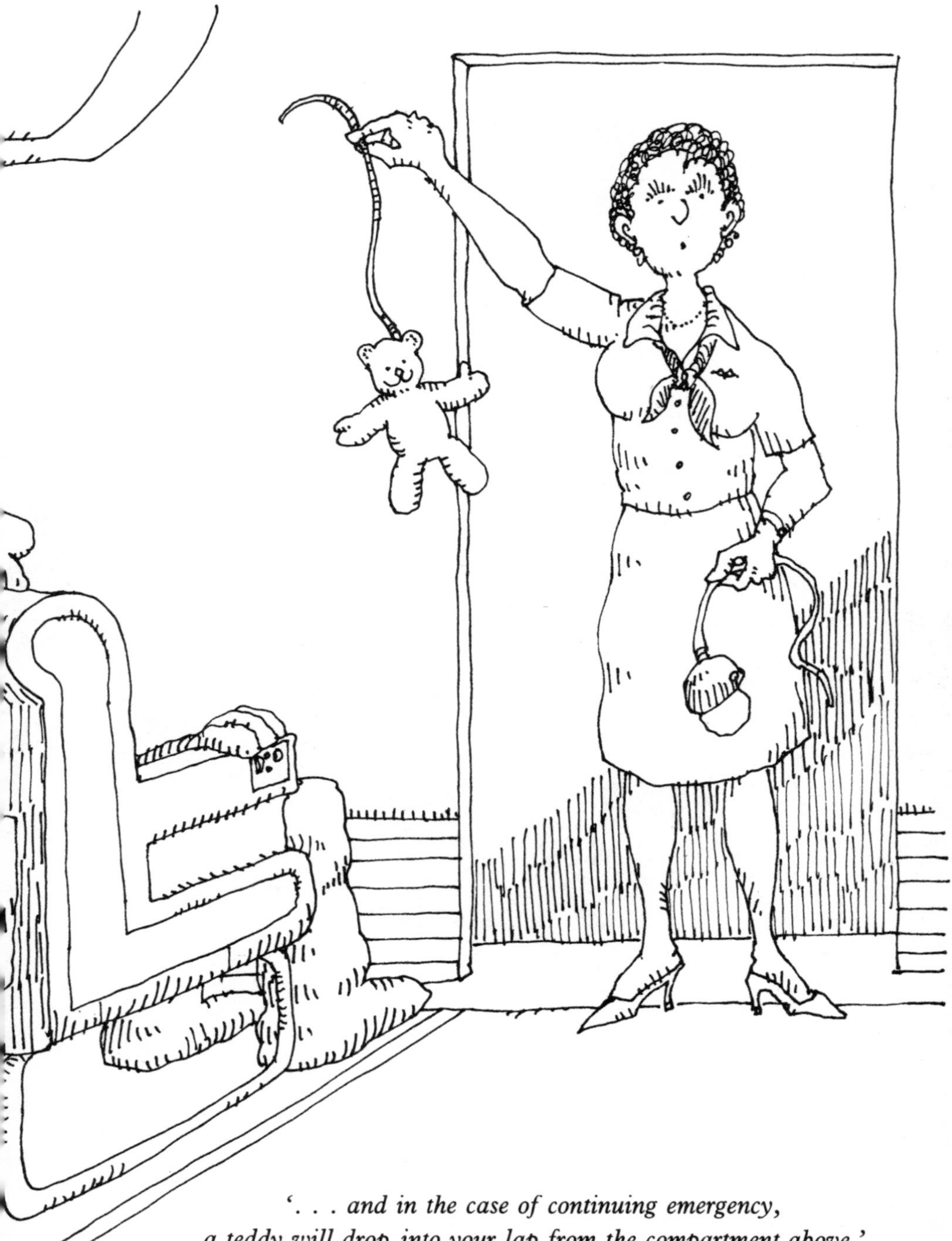

'. . . and in the case of continuing emergency,
a teddy will drop into your lap from the compartment above.'

THE END OF INNOCENCE...

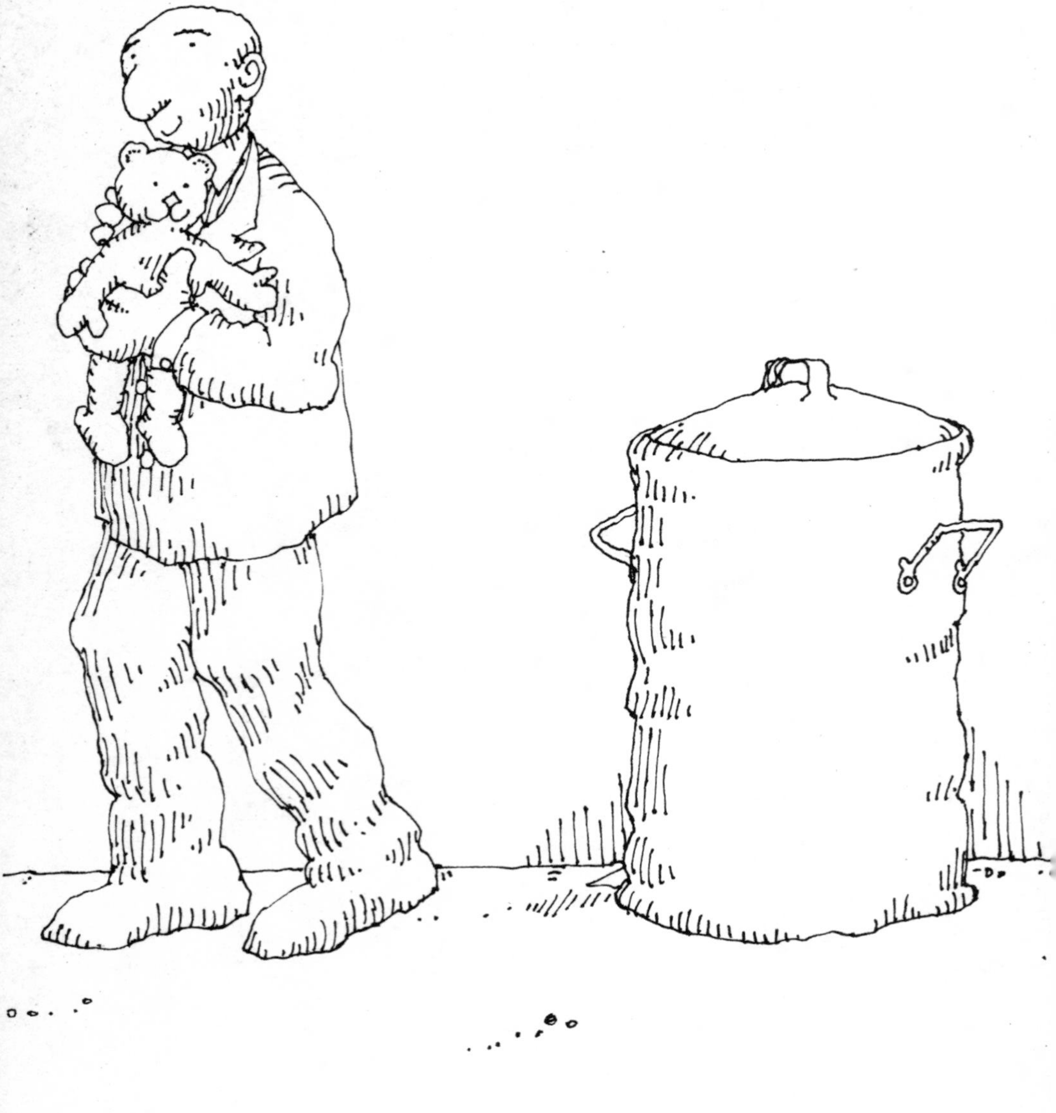

. . . but in the end love conquers all.